The Christian Apprehension of God

The
Christian Apprehension of God

BY

H. R. MACKINTOSH

D.PHIL., D.D., NEW COLLEGE
EDINBURGH

WIPF & STOCK · Eugene, Oregon

Wipf and Stock Publishers
199 W 8th Ave, Suite 3
Eugene, OR 97401

The Christian Apprehension of God
By Mackintosh, H. R.
ISBN 13: 978-1-60608-188-4
Publication date 12/02/2008
Previously published by Student Christian Movement Press, 1929

PREFACE

The following chapters, virtually in their present form, were delivered in March 1928, as Lectures on the James Sprunt Foundation, at the Union Theological Seminary, Richmond, Virginia. In printing them I wish to express my warm thanks to the authorities of the Seminary for their singular kindness to me during my stay in their famed and delectable city.

It may be advisable to add that the Lectures were addressed to a general rather than to a specially theological audience. I mention this not in order to forestall criticism, but to explain why an endeavour was naturally made to keep within limits the discussion of points of technical theology. It would be easy to name various relevant topics which have either been wholly omitted, or handled with a brevity quite incommensurate with their real importance. My object in this book is to give what the general reader may perhaps find to be a fairly intelligible, and not too detailed, treatment of the Christian apprehension of God, in the light of present-day thought.

H. R. MACKINTOSH.

NEW COLLEGE, EDINBURGH,
 14*th May* 1929.

THE JAMES SPRUNT LECTURES

In 1911 Mr James Sprunt of Wilmington, North Carolina, gave to the Trustees of Union Theological Seminary in Virginia the sum of thirty thousand dollars, since increased by his generosity to fifty thousand dollars, for the purpose of establishing a perpetual Lectureship, which would enable the Institution to secure from time to time the services of distinguished ministers and authoritative scholars, outside the regular Faculty, as special Lecturers on subjects connected with various departments of Christian thought and Christian work. The Lecturers are chosen by the Faculty of the Seminary and a Committee of the Board of Trustees, and the Lectures are published after their delivery in accordance with a contract between the Lecturer and these representatives of the Institution. The seventeenth series of Lectures on this Foundation is presented in this volume.

B. R. LACY, Jr.
President.

UNION THEOLOGICAL SEMINARY
IN VIRGINIA.

CONTENTS

CHAPTER		PAGE
I.	The Nature of Religion	9
II.	The Special Character of Religious Knowledge	36
III.	The Idea of Revelation	64
IV.	The Biblical Conception of God	92
V.	The Personality of God	118
VI.	The Holiness of God	144
VII.	The Love of God	171
VIII.	The Sovereign Purpose of God	199
	Index	231

The Christian Apprehension of God

CHAPTER I

THE NATURE OF RELIGION

IN the following chapters attention will be directed, though with no pretension to exhaustiveness, upon some important aspects of the Christian apprehension of God. The mere announcement of such a topic, it might appear, must savour of presumption, for we cannot speak worthily of the Ineffable. Yet it is misleading to disqualify or prohibit all positive statements concerning God, on the ground that such minds as ours are incapable of grasping His infinite being, and that our best worship of Him, accordingly, is silence. This has been depicted as the most reverent attitude of all; in presence of One who by definition is incomprehensible we had best say nothing. The suggestion has a convincing look, but only at first sight. Two considerations, to adduce no more, may be urged in rejoinder.

In the first place, while God is unfathomable, He is not unknowable, otherwise Jesus could not have said: " He that hath seen me hath seen the Father " ; nor could the Apostle have written: " God is love." These great declarations obviously imply that in some positive degree God can be known and characterized. It is true to say that

God is of a certain nature, and that this nature is one which the human mind can apprehend. He is love; He is *not* either hate or indifference. The whole idea of revelation falls to pieces unless we are justified in believing that knowledge of God is not intrinsically out of the question. In revealing Himself God takes the initiative in calling us to know Him, and to rejoice in the knowledge thus made ours.

The second consideration is one which no one tolerably well acquainted with history could lightly put aside. It is that true statements about God are necessary to refute and expel statements which are false. Unless God has a real character, which means one thing and does not mean its opposite, and unless the truth can be put in words and conveyed from one mind to another, we have no safeguard against ideas concerning God which are grotesque, trivial, or sheerly contradictory, or which, though not perhaps wholly unsound, are yet on an appreciably lower level than those derived from Jesus Christ. In short, good theology is the only thing that will keep out bad. The anarchist, to whom all government is anathema, can only be successfully encountered in argument if we start with some clarified notion of what is meant by "ordered human society" as a vital element in civilization. The not altogether uncommon person who argues that all sorts of education have an equal value, or even that no education is best of all, can be answered only if we have in our minds some definite conception,

THE NATURE OF RELIGION

not, of course, complete, but true so far as it goes, of what it means to have an educated mind. Purely negative ideas on these subjects, or the refusal to speak about them, give no help. Similarly, the mere abstention from definite affirmations about God contributes nothing to the refutation and expulsion of thoughts of the Divine which, if taken seriously, have in the past exerted an influence on human life which it would be no exaggeration to describe as poisonous. For antiseptic purposes, then, we need a view of God which is positive and searching; a view that not merely commends itself by its own coherence and sublimity, but acts as a touchstone by which to detect inadequacy or falsehood.

To speak of " the Christian apprehension of God," therefore, is a thoroughly Christian thing to do. In using this phrase we make no claim to omniscience. There was perhaps a time when theologians were supposed to know everything, and could speak impressively *de omnibus rebus et quibusdam aliis;* but that day is far behind us now. To-day, taught by psychology, we are ready to confess that we know comparatively little either about ourselves or others. For my part, I have sympathy with the man who said he found so much difficulty in understanding the moods of his next-door neighbour that he listened with a smile of incredulous wonder to historians who undertook to explain to him the innermost motives of Tiglath-pileser. How much less could we " find out the Almighty unto perfection ! " We cannot be too lowly-minded in our proposal to describe God, the Holy One, who inhabits eternity. Yet it is not for nothing that Christ is named the Light of the world. He is the Light because, as the Fourth Evangelist expresses it : " He has brought the Father out to view."[1] When we let Christ show us God, when we speak out to others the thoughts of God which come to us under Christ's influence, we are obeying the impulse of His Spirit.

It is convenient to begin with a short survey of the nature of Religion, and there is good reason why we should do so. The suggestion is constantly being made by people whose acquaintance with the subject is far from intimate, that religion could quite well subsist apart from beliefs of any kind. It could dispense even with beliefs about God. But religion without a God is hardly more impressive than that other modern curiosity—psychology without a soul. It recalls the American statesman who, as his biographer narrates, once sent out notices to his friends to say that he was going to be married, but without mentioning to whom. If we inquire briefly into the nature of religion as such, its vital characteristics and constituents, we shall find, I think, that convictions about the Divine have virtually always formed one of its living factors.

By speaking of " religion as such " we imply that other forms of religion than Christianity have

[1] John i. 18.

THE NATURE OF RELIGION

existed and still exist. The fact that we use the word "religions" in the plural, and that no people has ever turned out to be wholly devoid of pious impulse and practice, impels us to reflect on the phenomena of religion as a whole, and to ask how they are related to the religion we believe in and reckon as supreme. Three centuries ago theology took a rather different line. In that age it was assumed that real religion exists only in Christianity. Such a view no doubt gives expression, however unsympathetically, to the certainty that Christian faith rests upon a perfect revelation, and in that sense is in a class by itself. But it takes no account of the fact that a certain psychological similarity, as well as a certain identity of aim, characterize all known forms of religion, in spite of their almost infinitely numerous differences in truth and value. We may naturally ask whether this sixteenth-century attitude to the study and appreciation of other faiths is not, at least partially, due to the circumstance that at the time little or nothing was being done for foreign missions. The Church had not then faced other worships. But to-day, the missionary addresses himself to his work in another spirit. To declare that Christianity *is* that which other religions are trying to be, viz., unhindered fellowship with God; or, to put it otherwise, that what man, as a religious being, has hitherto been striving after in myriad forms, has been *given* him completely and finally in Jesus Christ—even this is scarcely enough, and would only imperfectly convey the modern difference of perspective. We prefer to follow St Paul in his contention that non-Christians also enjoy Divine revelation; they recognize God's invisible being through His visible works; they recognize His voice in conscience. In other words, outside Christianity more is to be observed than a fruitless search on the part of unaided man for the Divine reality; there has been a positive self-disclosure of God. We cannot but relate *all* the phenomena of man's religious history to a vast redeeming Divine plan. We can say nothing less than that there has been proceeding an "education of the human race" up to, and in, fellowship with God —such an education as found its climax in the sending of God's Son and the bestowal of God's Spirit. This, and only this, brings Christianity into a positive relation to the other great worships. As it has been put: "These religions are not Christianity, they are not equivalents for Christianity, but they are at least manifestations of that in man to which Christianity makes appeal; and it would be an artificial and timid construction of Christianity that did not do what it could to appreciate them and determine its own relation to them."

Investigation of the history and inner structure of the religions of mankind has been going on briskly for at least a century. Enough is now ascertained to enable us to answer one or two cardinal questions with a tolerable degree of insight.

First, what *is* religion in its intrinsic essence?

THE NATURE OF RELIGION

When we speak of "the scientific attitude" or "the moral attitude," every one attaches to these phrases a fairly distinct meaning. So, too, there is such a thing as "the religious attitude"; and it is desirable that the significance of this phrase also should be determined as exactly as possible. It should be marked off clearly from the other chief ways in which man confronts, and reacts to, the facts of his experience. Probably the word "religion" itself will not tell us much. Language, as we have it in life or literature, has drifted far away from the primitive meaning of its constituent parts; and a mere word is a locked drawer until we open it with the key of history.

What is religion? Conceivably we might set about answering the question by simple logic. We might say: What God is, is known; what man is, is also known: if we look closely at both we shall be able to tell by inspection what religion must be, since it is the essential relationship between them. Once this method may have had defenders, but they now are few. All are agreed that we cannot make up a definition of religion out of our heads, or by adding ideas together; our definition must be gathered out of the concrete facts. To fix what religion must be and is merely by thinking hard is as impracticable as to deduce electricity from our inner consciousness. The answer to our problem lies involved in the great religions which have won and held the suffrages of mankind.

The opinion has also been put forward that we

may decide the question of the essential nature of religion by fixing the "greatest common factor" that enters into all the existent faiths. Let us construct this maximum of elements common to Christianity, Buddhism, Judaism, Shintoism, Confucianism, and so forth; and when we have got it, *that* will be the essence we are seeking. This is, in fact, the procedure which Herbert Spencer recommends as the right way to find out the truth in such a case. But the objections are too strong to be overruled. For one thing, it is an arithmetical method which compels us to treat all religions as of equal importance; for arithmetic has no favourites, and Christianity and Shintoism must each count as one, neither as more than one. Besides, let us suppose that the hoped-for "greatest common factor" has been extracted. Quite clearly, it would be so vague and exiguous that the task of finding language sufficiently indefinite to express it would be one of insuperable difficulty. You cannot *name* a colour made up of all the colours there are. We must try some other way. An abstract statement of all the common characteristics belonging to every known worship, whether existing or obsolete or imagined as yet to be, is worthless for our purpose.

What we really want at this stage is not so much a merely obscure and indistinct formulation of the kind just indicated as a dynamic conception of the living tendency which, with more or less fullness and definiteness, is operative in all religions. The

THE NATURE OF RELIGION

essence of religion cannot have remained unchanged throughout human history; if, therefore, it is to be described effectively, we must conceive it not as stationary and immutable, but rather as analogous to a seed that grows and unfolds, becoming richer and fuller with the lapse of time. It is a vital impulse that moves forward and develops in ever new modes. We had better say "describe effectively" than "define"; for by define we are apt to mean formulating the meaning of the thing in question in terms not themselves implying the thing's own special qualities. And in this sense there is much to be said for the contention that religion neither needs nor admits of strict definition. For religion begins with religion, not with something else. Even so, however, we can point to instances of it which would be disputed by no one; so that our failure to supply a precise definition need not perturb us greatly.

But at this preliminary stage it may be said: You are considering other religions than Christianity, but must not the fact that you profess and call yourself a Christian disqualify you from understanding and estimating them fairly? Are not your Christian convictions, from this point of view, mere prejudices? The answer is that at the moment we are not investigating the truth or value of this or that religion; we are simply trying to find out what religion is; and our interest is not at present directed to what makes Christianity different from other faiths, but to what makes it like them. So long as we are merely searching for facts, we may begin where we like; and in Christian faith as such there is presumably nothing which disqualifies any one from recognizing facts.

Modern investigation, it is safe to say, has enabled us to make one or two quite definitely descriptive statements about religion,[1] wherever it occurs. Let it be again emphasized that we are dealing simply with a living tendency, not a rigidly connected complex of factors; for it would be difficult to point to any single characteristic, institutional, ritual, dogmatic or ethical, which unfailingly reappears in every instance. Assuming this, it may be broadly stated that religion is dependent faith in spiritual beings or powers, or in a spiritual being or power, superior over man and the world, together with the felt need to have personal fellowship therewith. Or in Warde

[1] In this chapter it is convenient to use terms which exhibit religion as an individual experience, but this must not be understood as a contention that religion is merely individualistic or private. So far from that, it is *essentially* social, from its lowest stage to its highest; it is enjoyed in, and constitutes, a specific form of society. As a common faith, it unites men in common experiences. In religion as in morality, the individual is what he is through a corporate relationship to others. Man is never alone in piety. We can follow this up into the supreme religion itself; for in the New Testament each member of the Body of Christ is necessary to all the rest. Most of the Christian virtues are meaningless except as manifested in the midst of a living community. In thus giving its imprimatur to the conception of religion as vitally not accidentally social, Christianity has only developed and lifted to perfection an element which has been central from the first.

THE NATURE OF RELIGION

Fowler's terser words : " Religion is the effective desire to be in right relationship to the power manifesting itself in the Universe." In virtually all known faiths which confront Christianity to-day there is a reaching out towards such a superhuman power or powers, together with the conviction that fuller and more satisfying life can thus be gained. These points are to be noted. First, there is an awareness of a " Supreme " or " Holy," apprehended as somehow disclosing its nature through the world and the course of human life, though not necessarily conceived as will and individual personality ; and here Otto has recently much strengthened the argument for holding that " the Divine " is immediately perceived and not merely inferred by reasoning. The believer takes its reality for granted. Secondly, in religion, man is conscious of certain grave difficulties which surround and trouble his life, of a kind which neither he nor his fellows unaided can remove. Thirdly, the thought is present of a blessing by which these difficulties can be overcome. And fourthly, some idea prevails, however rudimentary, of a way or method by which this life-giving value or blessing can be secured.

We ought not to miss the fact that " Deity " is conceived as possessing what we can only call " will," of at least partially moral character, as being interested in the lot of man, and as bearing towards worshippers such a relationship that they are not only dependent on the Supreme but responsible to it. In other words, no conception of religion can be right which regards it as practised exclusively for the sake of favours to come. From the first, a recognition prevails that fellowship with the Divine is desirable on its own account, apart from benefits. Hence the familiar argument that faith is a mere wish, and God our own shadow flung upon the clouds, involves a confusion of issues. Wishes undoubtedly have to do with the genesis of faith, but the deeper question still remains behind: Why were these wishes felt? Are they like the plant stretching out its tendrils to fresh water? May they not point to a profound affinity between man and God? In that case the wish reveals itself as the soul's response to the dimly-felt presence of the God it needs. A certain kind of book on the psychology of religion ought to be read with distrust; I mean the kind where the writer professes only to be reporting on faith as a psychologist, but really indulges in arrogant dogmatism. Often his object is simply to explain how men come to see the particular sort of mirage which they name " God."

The criticism has been made that if in religion we include, as a vital element, the belief in superhuman Divinity, we thereby disqualify Buddhism; for is not primitive Buddhism an instance of a religion without a god? But in fact—though the possibility of a " godless " religion is not hastily to be denied—it is more than doubtful whether Buddhism would have survived as anything more than a high type of morality, or a philosophy, unless it had gradually made room for belief in

THE NATURE OF RELIGION

God and immortality by deifying Gautama and transforming Nirvana into something more positive than a mere absence of desire.[1] In a way the same thing has occurred in Confucianism, which by itself is just a moral system, not really a religion. Yet well-informed people tell us that in the strict sense Confucianism *became* a religion only the other day, when Confucius was publicly constituted a god by edict of the Chinese Government.

It is of interest to ask how religion is differentiated from science and art. Clearly enough, religion and science resemble each other in this respect, that both insist on going behind mere appearance, beyond the superficial sequences of events, in order to seize the deeper ground of change, and thereby explain or cast light on the course of things. But by " explaining," each means a different type of thought. The impulse to explain which moves the religious man is fundamentally unlike that which animates the scientific worker. It is not merely that the mood of the scientific man is one of detachment, while the believer has a passionate interest in the truth of his beliefs about God. In addition, the scientist

[1] Apart from this, it has been well pointed out that " Buddhism is certainly more than merely a moral theory inculcating a manner of life. Like all religion, it bases its teaching of salvation on a definite theory of, and attitude towards, the universe as a whole, and its inexorable law of Karma has for a Buddhist's life and thought much of the meaning which God has for a Christian's " (Hoernle, *Matter, Mind, Life and God*, p. 169).

seeks to explain the processes of Nature by detailing and inter-relating the causes by which these processes are produced, but what the religious man wants to know is that, whatever the processes may be, they are under Divine control and serve a Divine purpose. Hence while science rightly is content with explanations that keep strictly within the boundaries of space and time, religion insists on rising up, beyond the world of phenomena, to a transcendent Power, and entering into fellowship with the Unseen. There is in it the thrill of response to the " supernatural."

In certain respects religion and art also are alike; in this, for example, that they both address themselves to the soul rather than the disinterested intelligence, and induce in us that deep blessed contemplative attitude of the inner life in which we feel ourselves elevated above the pain and dispeace of the world, and there is unveiled before us " the ideal of a fairer, nobler, more complete and harmonious life than the common eye can discern in the world of our ordinary experience." Art has lent to religion its outward vesture; religion has supplied the artist with his loftiest themes. We can scarcely be surprised, therefore, that it should have been said: Religion is simply love of the beautiful. Yet it is not difficult to see that in their ultimate meaning religion and art are widely different. Thus, art raises no question concerning the objective truth of its creations. Who cares whether Shakespeare's Cordelia or Desdemona ever lived? Who asks how long ago

THE NATURE OF RELIGION

the incidents of Virgil's *Aeneid* took place ? It is enough if a work of art be charged with something of timeless and universal beauty. Art need not canvass the problem of ultimate truth, for it makes no claim to rule our lives ; its appeal is to the æsthetic sense, not to the entire personality. But religion confronts us with the holy, the august, the unconditionally sublime and commanding; here, accordingly, the question of objective truth is vital and inescapable.

By most present-day investigators it is agreed that the basal impulses behind religion are more practical than theoretic, and that the needs which religion comes to satisfy are not those of the analytic intellect but those of man as a living whole. Are these practical needs invariably moral, at least in part ? Is it the fact that even the most primitive religion is shot through with moral elements ? The question is important, and the difficulty of replying to it largely derives from the obscurity surrounding all origins. Since the lowest religions are the least known, it is a wholly unscientific assumption that they may not represent a declension from higher forms of worship. At the same time, unless we are bent on dividing up human experience into water-tight compartments, we certainly shall lean to the view that religion and morality have always been in some real degree interwoven, and that from the first religion embraced ethical factors which influence both its conception of Deity and the conduct of the devotee. Even the *tabu-mana* system of the

THE CHRISTIAN APPREHENSION OF GOD

Polynesians contains, however vaguely and crudely, the idea that duty is unconditionally valid. " In its rudest forms," Robertson Smith has said, " religion was a moral force, the powers that man reveres were on the side of social order and tribal law, and the fear of the gods was a motive to enforce the laws of society, which were also the laws of morality."[1] In short, the needs satisfied by religion are not accidental to life; they are essential. They are needs felt not simply because man's position in this weary, unintelligible world is shadowed and perilous, but because man as man is what he is. Behind the ever-varied strivings by which he seeks to obtain the higher goods there lies a dim consciousness that he is born for infinite things, there moves an inextinguishable longing for perfect life; and this longing, this consciousness, impels him to unite himself to the loftiest kind of supramundane Power which the existing stage of his development has enabled him to conceive.

That religion is universal—not in the sense that every individual human being is religious, but that religion is found everywhere throughout history—may be taken as ascertained fact. For a time this was doubted, or even, in some quarters, denied. A generation ago, Lubbock committed himself to the verdict that so far from religion being universal, a considerable number of tribes showed no trace of it. His error was due to the hasty

[1] *Religion of the Semites* (Revised Edition), p. 53.

observation of a few missionaries, but chiefly of not unduly sympathetic travellers. We now know that primitive peoples are apt to conceal their religion from visitors, not because they are ashamed of it (a feeling apparently confined to Christians), but because the stranger is deemed unworthy to behold the sacred mysteries. They are shy and unwilling to speak of religious matters. They fob off the white man with explanations which they think may give him pleasure and forestall more searching inquiries. Even when he does speak, the savage may be misunderstood. The traveller comes to investigation with a certain pigeon-hole in his mind labelled " religion," and if the primitive practices will not fit into this orifice, they are cast aside. Or it may be that his knowledge of the native speech is extremely imperfect, or that his interpreter serves him badly. It is a wholly unfounded view that there are tribes or peoples quite devoid of religion. Atheism is a relatively modern product, and the attempt to place it near the outset of the human development would not now be repeated by any serious scholar.

Let us now turn to the psychological character or structure of religion. Take a man in the specifically religious attitude : what are the ideas, feelings, volitions, present in his mind and behaviour ? Or to go still further back, does he have ideas or beliefs; can the whole be described solely in terms of feeling ? Is the will operative, or does the will reserve itself for morality ? Such distinctions have been proposed, but the closer our scrutiny, the less possible do we find it to fix on any one psychical function as exclusively involved. What psychologists regard as the three ultimate modes of being conscious—the feeling attitude, the knowing attitude, the willing or striving attitude—are all present in a religious experience; and they function as a living unity. You cannot have an act of worship without the recognition of an adored object with which the worshipper is in relation: this is knowledge. Nor is worship possible without the emotions of fear, yearning or grateful love: this is feeling. Nor, finally, can worship be offered without some sort of activity generated by such feeling, whether the activity be outward, like sacrifice, or inward, like prayer: this is willing.[1] All three are fused in one vital moment. They are not successive but simultaneous and interdependent.

Religion, then, as self-surrender to the Supreme (however the Supreme be conceived), involves each of the three chief forms or manifestations of mental life. The Supreme for feeling is the Highest Good, to which all other goods are subordinate, and are felt as less creative of bliss. To the will the Supreme is the Highest Power, which puts all other forces beneath itself. To knowledge the Supreme is the Highest or Absolute Reality, which makes all other realities merely relative and by

[1] See Adams Brown, *Christian Theology in Outline*, p. 30.

THE NATURE OF RELIGION

comparison utterly minor. All three combine in the attitude of piety.

As we might anticipate, frequent efforts have been made to secure something like a monopoly for one of these three factors. Thus, to take the best known instance, Schleiermacher is disposed to refer religion exclusively to the domain of feeling—the feeling, as he phrases it, of absolute or unqualified dependence. Hegel, construing religion as a sort of kindergarten metaphysic, has intellectualized religion unduly by giving primary importance to the element of knowledge; this may also be said of Croce, the distinguished Italian thinker, to whom religion is just philosophy speaking in parables. Kant, who defined religion with a certain narrowness as "the recognition of all duties as divine commands," thus virtually reducing religion to morality and ignoring everything that can be called fellowship with God, may be taken as an example of the third class, that which identifies piety with action. But these departmental views of what religion is have not worn well. They are not corroborated by experience. The same inexorable touchstone condemns every new attempt to leave out any one of the three strands in the cord. It is unnecessary to work this out in detail; but we are safe in affirming that religion without an element of knowledge would sink to the level of magic; without feeling, it would be heartless formalism; without will, it would justly incur the charge of exerting an anti-moral and even anti-social influence.

Each of the three factors merits separate study. To take ideas first:[1] in most quarters a strong tendency has shown itself to distinguish clearly between belief in spirits or demons, and belief in gods or God—religion only beginning when gods are believed in.[2] Along with this goes a firmer differentiation between religion and magic; the contrast, even for scholars who hold that both sprang from a common stem, amounting to this, that magic endeavours to "manage" the gods, to utilise and bend them even against their will, but religion worships, and the worshipper is filled with reverence. Not only so, but gods as distinct from spirits stand much closer to man, though superficially they might seem further off; at least up to a point they have the ability and disposition to do him good. Brinton lays down that "the early gods are more or less friendly towards men," and Andrew Lang describes them as "fathers in heaven and friends, guardians of morality." The point is one on which a shifting of opinion is observable in recent discussion; and it is of interest to have it acknowledged, even by thinkers who would not themselves claim to be religious men, that religion and magic are not the same thing.

In regard to feelings or emotions there has been

---

[1] In religion the intellect goes hand in hand with imagination and clothes ideas in symbolic vestures.

[2] But belief in *mana* (see p. 32) is itself prior to animism, which though probably from its rise allied with religion is not necessarily in itself religious at all.

THE NATURE OF RELIGION

in some degree a parallel change in sympathetic and scholarly opinion. The old naturalistic tradition, derived through Hume and Comte from the ancient Epicureans, taught that in religion the dominant emotion is fear. Spencer, for instance, holds that religious laws spring from fear of the dead. There is truth in this emphasis on fear, though truth of a one-sided and misleading type; for in religion reverence is fundamental, and reverence includes fear and love together. Besides, it is shallow to imagine that fear necessarily is craven or ignoble. If I fear to do wrong, because if I offend I shall forfeit the respect of those I venerate, injure my neighbours, and lose touch with God, my fear is nothing to be ashamed of; on the contrary, it forms part of a perfectly right attitude in the circumstances, and religion would be poorer, not richer, if it were away. The man who merely stands erect in God's presence, unaware of any need to bend in awe before the Holy One, the "Determiner of Destiny," has misconceived religion. But true fear is no slavish terror that shatters and paralyses, it is elevating and transfiguring; and something of the same quality, we may well believe, goes back to the beginnings. Hence it is not surprising that among modern investigators the voices are becoming more numerous which proclaim that not mere terror but confidence, trust and love are the preponderating feelings by which religion as such is characterized. Robertson Smith's words have often been quoted. "From the earliest times,"

THE CHRISTIAN APPREHENSION OF GOD

he writes, " religion, as distinct from magic or sorcery, addresses itself to kindred and friendly beings, who may indeed be angry with their people for a time, but are always placable except to the enemies of their worshippers or to renegade members of the community."[1] Jevons, another expert, underlines this, going so far as to say that all real religion is rooted not in fear but in love. As we have seen, there is no reason why we should deny that fear, in a reverential sense, does form an ingredient in the emotional nidus of religion, and that the factor is one which can never be eliminated without loss. But, assuming this, it is important to observe that here we have a point at which inquirers starting from an examination of Nature-religions are gradually approximating to the description of typically religious feelings which would be offered by, say, members of the theological school of Ritschl or psychologists in general sympathy with William James. Once again it is satisfactory to be told by people who can fairly claim to be disinterested investigators, that the feeling in which religion especially strikes root is not that of fear in its lower significance, but rather reverence and trust, with their literally infinite potencies of development.

As for the third element in mental life, striving or volition, we can be brief. It is being more and more widely acknowledged that from the most distant times accessible to inquiry, religion has acted as a moral force. Feeling sets the will in

[1] *Religion of the Semites*, p. 54.

THE NATURE OF RELIGION

motion; and the volitions stimulated by religious feeling are, at least in part, of an ethical character. No religion has been without a real striving to attain what is felt to be the supreme good, or without a readiness to relate this striving somehow to the superhuman powers—a simple consideration which of itself links up religion alike with morality and culture. It is not merely that the consciousness of a higher will goes to curb selfishness and thus promote ethical discipline; in addition, religion exerts a quickening influence on the social conscience, rudimentary as this conscience may be. In primitive circles, men are often spared from slaughter or helped in need from motives almost wholly religious.

The origin of religion lies buried in obscurity. Certain ethnologists have laboured under the calamitous delusion that the lowest and least developed Nature-religions now extant afford a fairly exact picture of religion in its earliest form, and that by inspection of these we can tell how religion as such originated. Little progress is to be expected by this track. Two generations ago it was a widespread hypothesis that the most primitive religion was that ramified belief in " souls " and " spirits " known as Animism;. this was countered later by the theory, also derived from a study of Nature-peoples, that religion to begin with was a primitive Monotheism; opposed to both now stands the contention, for which the evidence is strong, that in its first form religion was the worship of a mysterious power or influence, often called "*mana*" and conceived as less or more personal—"*mana*" being, in the words of one investigator, "what works to effect everything which is beyond the ordinary power of men, outside the common processes of nature." This is a region in which assured knowledge is obviously hard to come by.

Perhaps even the search for it is apt to conceal from us the greater importance of a simpler inquiry: What are the permanent and basal motives of all religion, in every age, our own included? We wish to understand not merely the genesis of religion millenniums ago, but why religion has its birth still, say, in our friends and contemporaries.[1] It is easy, if this larger issue be overlooked, to derive the religious consciousness from experiences which belong solely to a particular period and are undergone only by persons existing at a very depressed plane of life. So it is when the evoking causes are said to be dreams, visions, or the sight of sleep or death. The most famous description of religion from this point of view is probably that of M. Salomon Reinach, who declares it to be "a collection of scruples which impede the free exercise of our faculties." Here the tacit assumption is that once religion has

---

[1] In his remarkable book, *The Interpretation of Religion* (1929), Professor John Baillie enumerates impressively various things which are, he says, "so certainly true as to put out of court any theory of religion which gives *one* explanation of its origin and *another* explanation of its present power" (p. 165).

THE NATURE OF RELIGION

fairly started, it will persist by the law of inertia until the initial superstitious impulse has spent itself and religion collapses, to make way for philosophy or science.

Thus the greater problem is, what calls forth religion in man yesterday, to-day, and for ever ? On one positive statement we may venture—man is religious because he needs to be. The need may in part be that of explaining the mysterious world where he finds himself, in part that of calling in superior aid to enable him to cope with natural or moral difficulties and dangers ; in part—and here we approach an idea of vast moment—the need of uniting himself to a Power which has in some degree evoked his trust and satisfied his yearning for fuller life through experiences of his inner life of feeling. But we cannot reflect long upon this perplexing question without realizing that to point to felt human need could not in itself be an ultimate explanation of religion. The deeper issue still remains behind—why is the need felt ? And to this believers in God can give only one reply. The feeling of need is a symptom that man is constituted for God, and that the impact and challenge of this great Presence lies upon him from the first. If religion is evoked by the necessities of our troubled and imperfect life, these necessities themselves bear witness to our kinship with the Divine.

Man, then, is susceptible to religion because of this underlying and ineradicable kinship; how or by what is the susceptibility made active ? In a word, by revelation. St Paul is here amazingly modern. He points first to Nature, as in a real degree reflecting the Divine character and unavoidably impressing the human mind. There is that within man, he declares, which so catches the meaning of all that is without as to issue in an actual apprehension of God. " The invisible things of Him since the creation of the world are clearly seen, being perceived through the things that are made, even His everlasting power and divinity."[1] Secondly, in his speech at Athens he brings out the moral significance of history : " He made of one every nation of men . . . having determined their appointed seasons, and the bounds of their habitation ; that they should seek God, if haply they might feel after Him and find him."[2] Here many of the best modern inquirers are ready to follow the Apostle. They too are unwilling to refer religion to a single evoking cause or stimulus ; they speak of such things as a social reaction to friendly nature-powers like the sunshine, but also of reaction to striking and phenomenal events. And it is in fact within these two realms of experience, Nature and History, that man encounters those objective facts which go alike to stimulate and to satisfy his longing for perfect life, and to convey the assurance that there exists a Superhuman Power (whether conceived as plural or singular), capable of bestowing the perfect boon thus longed for.

For Christian thought, the religiously complete

[1] Rom. i. 20. [2] Acts xvii. 26-27.

THE NATURE OF RELIGION

revelation of God in Jesus Christ is the confirmation of all that is good and prophetic in lesser forms of faith, however rudimentary. By His very meaning Christ is proof that in religion, right on from its lowest stages, man has not been stretching out his hands into a universe empty, blind, and deaf. Rather at every point he has been responding to the touch of a God who creates the higher longing, and in anticipating love stirs our prayer. In words we cannot quote too often, since they are final: " Thou hast made us for thyself, and our hearts are restless till they find rest in Thee."

CHAPTER II

THE SPECIAL CHARACTER OF RELIGIOUS KNOWLEDGE

THE subject with which we are concerned in these pages is the Christian apprehension of God. We began by treating cursorily of the question what religion is, as interpreted by some of the best modern inquirers in that general field ; and in the course of our study it became clear how impossible to square with the facts any theory of religion is which does not regard it as involving or embracing some kind of knowledge, some belief or conviction respecting " Deity," and the relation of Deity to man. The religious act or attitude is not merely a knowing act or attitude, otherwise it would be hard to distinguish it from science or philosophy. But knowledge is a living element in it, interlaced with feeling and volition. And the people who in the past have counted for most in religious progress have been the thinkers—not the mystics who lose themselves in ecstasies of feeling, nor the practical men, whose one aim is to get things done ; but the prophets and thinkers. The men who best understood religion and revealed in it new power to conquer the world, have been figures like Origen, Augustine, and Luther. It was a great conviction, or a body of great convictions resting on and revolving round a rediscovered Jesus Christ, that made the Reformation. It was a certain kind of

CHARACTER OF RELIGIOUS KNOWLEDGE

knowledge of God, not of course absolutely new, but newly caught up again from the Gospel of the New Testament.

Hence it is important that we should go on to study the peculiar nature of religious knowledge. In order to discuss with profit the Christian apprehension of God, we must first have tried to understand the special character of religious knowledge as such, the special ways by which we reach religious certainty, and the special kind of proof which is appropriate to religious truth. This is a topic, as is well known, on which long and interesting debate was held throughout the nineteenth century; it cannot indeed fail in any age to fascinate those who care deeply for religion.

Let us start from a position about which there is likely to be wide agreement. For Christian minds, religious knowledge means first and foremost that knowledge of spiritual reality, and supremely of God, which we have through *faith*. There is no such thing as faith, in the New Testament sense of the word, which does not imply conviction or (as we may say) heartfelt belief. And the first thing which deserves to be emphasized, since the point is one often left obscure in discussions of the matter, is this, that faith claims uncompromisingly to possess a real knowledge of its object. It is apprehending facts, not inventing them; it is sure that it is not merely on the pathway to reality, but has actually come in contact with the last and highest reality in the universe. "We know what we worship," our Lord said to the Samaritan woman. "I know whom I have believed," St Paul wrote, when his hard-fought conflict was nearly over. For centuries one attempt after another has been made to persuade the believer that he lives in a world of dreams, and that he would be very much happier and stronger and freer were he only prepared to acknowledge this, and cast his creed aside. But believers have repelled the charge. Indeed, it has often been through the battle with doubt and negation, rising in his own heart or suggested by the secularism of his age, that the man of faith has gained a more vigorous and personal conviction, as well as a new power to support and guide those whose feet were stumbling on the mountains of darkness. "I am persuaded," he answers to every objection that would rob him of saving and triumphant certainties. To give up the knowledge of faith would be to give up God.

Occasionally, in the name of extreme mysticism, it has been proposed to abandon the claim to knowledge, and to retreat into the citadel of personal feeling as into a sanctuary where, though all the enemies of piety smite upon the gate, they cannot enter or disturb the peace within. In many cases, of course, feeling when thus put forward as a solvent of all difficulties, is only knowledge under another name. In any case it *involves* knowledge. As has been pointed out, "Emotion itself implies an already existing belief; however the belief be arrived at (whether by tradition, imagination, authority, inference true

CHARACTER OF RELIGIOUS KNOWLEDGE

or false), the emotion implies that the intellectual belief is already there. Destroy that belief, and it goes. The biographies of those who have given up the religion of their childhood are full of testimony to that effect."[1] But apart from this, when people speak of "feeling" in this connexion, as often as not what they mean is not merely an emotion moving purely within the mind itself, and unrelated to any confronting object; it is rather an emotional type of knowledge. And in this wide though strictly inexact sense we have no quarrel with their contention. If, on the other hand, a man should say that he possesses God in feeling pure and simple, and that knowledge is here a foreign and positively injurious element, we are entitled, I think, to cross-examine him closely. We have a right to say: On what grounds are you justified in saying that what you thus possess exclusively in feeling is *God?* May it not be simply an inner state, a condition of your own soul in its ups and downs? How do you distinguish God from any other kind of emotional content? Or, to raise another but nearly related point, how could one who staked all on feeling and disclaimed all knowledge give help to a friend perplexed by doubts of God's existence? Without in the least claiming that God's reality can be proved to demonstration, there are two things you can do even on the intellectual plane—you can offer good grounds in reason for clinging to faith in God, and secondly (though this perhaps is the same general

[1] Rashdall, *Ideas and Ideals*, p. 9 f.

consideration in a different guise), you can show that negation has much bigger problems on its hands than faith, so that difficult as faith may be, unfaith is still more difficult. But you cannot urge either of these arguments if knowledge of God is intrinsically impossible. Hence the consequences of eliminating knowledge in religion and putting everything in terms of feeling are so grave that the purely mystical position can hardly be maintained, except on the assumption that the communication of religious truth from one mind to another is out of the question. Nor is the contention that God is utterly unknowable at all so reverent as it may sound. It looks very devout to argue that God is so great, so sublime, so ineffable that He is utterly beyond the reach of human apprehension, but the doctrine has implications very often overlooked. It limits the power of God in a preposterous degree. For obviously it implies that God cannot *reveal* Himself to man, cannot get through to the human spirit; and this is quite incredible if the God we believe in is real and wise and loving.

Faith, then, is convinced that it is in possession of genuine knowledge concerning God; but the knowledge it lays claim to is not of a scientific kind. Not that it covets scientific knowledge, but is reluctantly compelled to admit that this cannot be had. On the contrary; science is irrelevant to the convictions by which the religious man lives and could make nothing of them one way or the other. There is no scientific way of discovering

CHARACTER OF RELIGIOUS KNOWLEDGE

or proving the love of God, the redeeming power of Christ, the forgiveness of sins, the hope of immortality. In short, there are more kinds of knowledge than one, in the sense that the human mind has more ways than one of approaching and appropriating truth. We acquire knowledge in one way as scientific thinkers, we acquire it in a different and equally valid way as religious believers.

Let us analyse this distinction. If with many good writers we say that science operates with theoretic judgments, faith with value-judgments, what does the difference amount to and involve ? Here is an admirable description of a theoretic judgment. " It is one that has as the ground of its validity the compulsion of perception or logical thought. Every scientific and every strictly philosophical judgment is theoretical in character. Starting from perceived particulars, the scientist, and, in a larger way, the philosopher, proceed to the general conception that reduces these particulars to unity and order ; and they reach their goal when the whole world of known fact is causally or logically connected in a single organic system. The proof that their construction corresponds with reality lies simply in this, its ability to exhibit the facts in their interrelation and unity. It follows that the certainty with which such a construction is held is a purely logical certainty."

Now, in one or two definite ways the knowledge involved in faith resembles this. In science and religion equally there is an apprehending mind, and there is an apprehended reality. In both cases it is natural to speak of *truth*—meaning by this term that our thinking holds good of objective fact, fact that is given or presented to us as something other than, and in that sense beyond or outside, our own mind. Mathematicians are sure it is untrue to say that two and two make five, and Christians are equally sure it is untrue to say that God is sinful. In faith, as in science, there is an objective reality to be known; for faith that reality is revelation, for physical science it is what may be called, broadly, Nature. And revelation, *i.e.* the self-disclosure of God in and through the facts of the world and of human experience, is as definitely presented to, but not created by, the knowing mind, as the natural world is presented to the scientific intelligence. Faith, as we have seen, is aware that it is occupied not with dreams or wishes but with facts; with God as made real, near and sure to us through His self-revealing activity. The theory is occasionally put forward—and may even gain temporary vogue—that religious doctrines claim and require no more than *poetic* truth; but theories of that character, it will be found, are invariably produced by people who are not themselves believers. They are meant to show how certain persons come to ascribe reality to the beautiful fancy to which they give the name "God." In short, they are theories made *for* believers, never *by* them.

Another resemblance may be stated thus. Knowledge in science and knowledge in personal

CHARACTER OF RELIGIOUS KNOWLEDGE

religion are similar in this respect, that of necessity both use symbolic thought. When we try to put in human language what Christ has taught us concerning God, when for example we speak of the Divine Father, or when we repeat the glorious language of the Book of Revelation descriptive of the heavenly life, it of course turns out that the terms in which we speak are thoroughly and incurably figurative. Originally they sprang out of the experience of embodied minds, and traces however attenuated of their origin in sense-perception cling to them to the end. But in this respect religion is very far from being peculiar. Science does exactly the same thing. For example, the technical conceptions of physics are at bottom refined images of perception. No one has ever been in direct visual or tactual relations with an electron ; the idea of an electron is none the worse for owing much to the scientific imagination, but the imagination of the most penetrating mind among the physicists has no materials to work upon except such as have been derived from sense experience. So far, accordingly, knowing in science and knowing in religious faith are pretty much upon a par. Any objection on the score of the part played by imagination which might be brought against the one would lie also against the other. And if it be said that science can verify and correct its symbols by deeper research, it may reasonably be answered that Christian faith can verify, correct, and recorrect *its* symbols, and has constantly done so, by going back at intervals and

THE CHRISTIAN APPREHENSION OF GOD

testing them by the revelation which called faith into being. Thus various figures once used to explain the saving effect of Christ's death, such as those involved in the theory long current and all but orthodox to the effect that " the humanity of Christ was the bait which the Devil, like a greedy fish, eagerly swallowed and so became impaled upon the hook of His Divinity," have gradually evoked abhorrence and been dropped because they were felt to be utterly out of keeping with the revealed character of God. To a large extent the progress of theology has consisted, and so far as can be seen will always consist, in the severest but also discerning criticism of the symbols familiar to past centuries. They have all to be tried by their fidelity to the mind of Christ.

So much, very briefly, for resemblances; now for differences between the two kinds of knowing. That differences do exist it is hardly possible to deny. A heartfelt religious conviction is not the same kind of thing, at least on a first inspection, as a cool and detached scientific theory. The grounds on which I am persuaded that God pardons sin are not precisely similar to those on which I am persuaded that the three interior angles of a triangle are equal to two right angles. If we take great religious seers of the past, like the Hebrew prophets, we never find them arriving at the apprehension of their truth by scientific or philosophical argumentation. They do not carefully weigh evidence or calculate probabilities. The truths they proclaim are not hypotheses to be tested by the method of trial and error. To borrow an illustration from William Law, we might say that if the scientific intelligence took upon itself to pronounce upon the reality of what in Christian thought is known as " regeneration," it would be as much out of its place as the eye that takes upon it to smell. What the prophets do rather is to perceive their truth intuitively, by spiritual insight or inference, however much they may seek to defend it by inductive reasoning should it be attacked; and the fact that their insight has been trained by the influence of God's Spirit working through the sometimes tragic experiences of their own lives, does not lessen one whit the immediacy of their spiritual perceptions. Not only so, but the certainty with which they hold their truth is not a logical but a moral or spiritual certainty. A logical certainty it is impossible to doubt, once the steps in the argument have been understood, but it is not in the least impossible to doubt the convictions about the character and action of God set forth in the preaching of Amos or Hosea. Indeed, our deepest religious affirmations are, to put it so, flung in the face of what seem the hard facts of the world. " Though he slay me, yet will I trust in him."[1] Let us note, however, that the absence of what I have called logical certainty does not at all mean that religious truth is held with a lesser degree of assurance. Thus no so-called proof of the moral character of God can be stated which may not be

[1] Job xiii. 15.

traversed without a breach of the laws of thought; yet devout men live and die in the conviction of His boundless and unchanging love.

The difference in the appeal made by scientific and religious truth respectively may be exhibited otherwise. It may be seen in the effect each has upon our spiritual being. The religious kind of truth satisfies our whole man as the scientific never could. There is a universality in the religious interest which contrasts sharply with the departmental character of science. Everything that grows out of, or into, morality is universal in appeal, but intellectual operations which leave conscience untouched and do not open the door into a new kind of moral experience have no purchase on the entire personality; not merely do they not engross the whole man but they do not affect all men. I may read with fascination as much as the unmathematical layman can understand of the physical structure of the atom, or the inner constitution of the stars, but what I learn scarcely bears on the man I am or ought to be, and with all its intellectual charm lies somewhat on the periphery of my deepest concern. As Newman said of the arguments in proof of God's reality, so we may say of the facts of physical science : " They do not warm or enlighten me; they do not take away the winter of my desolation, or make my moral being rejoice." When face to face with temptation, or in perplexity over the meaning of this strange world, it is elsewhere I must go for light and strength.

CHARACTER OF RELIGIOUS KNOWLEDGE

It looks, then, as if the difference we are treating of were a real difference. Try as we may, we cannot eliminate the distinction between a kind of knowing that implies the recognition of independent moral values, and one that need not. Naturally there has been long and intense discussion regarding the precise formulation of the matter, and it would be untrue to say that anything like universal agreement has been reached. One promising contribution, however, has been made by the group of thinkers who have worked out what may in general terms be designated as the theory of value-judgments in religion. In some degree this special interpretation of religious knowledge goes back to Kant and Schleiermacher; some help in elucidating it was given by Lotze, who understood religion as on the whole few philosophers have done; but it is to Ritschl and some followers of his, notably Kaftan and Herrmann, that the prominence attained by the conception in recent thought is mainly due. It is not the case, as some opponents of this point of view appear to think, that the Ritschlians invented " value-judgments." Their presence and importance in other fields than religion had long been recognized, especially in the field of ethics. As it has been put: " There is a distinction between a judgment *of* fact and a judgment *upon* fact, corresponding to the distinction between " judgment " in its logical sense of " proposition " and " judgment " in its judicial sense of " sentence." A simple example may make this clear. In the proposition "the massacre of St Bartholomew took place in 1572" we have a simple judgment of fact; it might be made by any historian, whatever his sympathies, and whether or not he had formed an opinion regarding its goodness or badness. But in the proposition "the massacre was an evil and savage crime" we have a judgment of value upon it, based upon the reaction which this particular historical event evokes in our feeling and active nature. It gives expression to the estimate we put upon the episode, considered not merely as an event in space and time but as an event suffused with moral and spiritual meaning. But it is of great importance to note that what we have described as the judgment of value asserts the *fact* of the massacre no less than the other judgment does. It means nothing at all unless the massacre really happened. If this be kept in mind, certain apparently damaging criticisms of the general view lose all force. Summing up, then, we may say that in contrast to theoretic judgments, or simple judgments of fact, those we are calling judgments of value are such as "have as the ground of their validity, not the compulsion of perception or of logical thought, but the fact that the object about which the judgment is made possesses for us, as beings endowed with feeling, desire, volition, a certain value or worth." That value of course may be either positive or negative, good or bad; but in asserting it we assert the reality both of the object and of the value it embodies. Neither is

CHARACTER OF RELIGIOUS KNOWLEDGE

created by our thought; each is simply found to exist.

Many present-day thinkers are prepared to make use of this approach to the interpretation of Christian knowledge. To choose a simple and unobjectionable instance, they would say that when a Christian declares that God is love, he does so supremely on the basis of the appeal made to his moral and spiritual susceptibilities by what he sees of love and redeeming power in Jesus Christ. That love and that power come home to his heart, and through the impression thus received his mind opens to faith in the Father. " Christ lived and died in Palestine 1900 years ago " is a historical statement which might be made by Mohammedan or Buddhist. But " God was in Christ reconciling the world to himself "[1] is a statement into which the believer has put that which Christ means to him personally. It brings out the worth and preciousness of Christ for faith. It expresses what the fact of Christ involves for sinful men. That fact has mastered and subdued us, it has made us the forgiven children of God, it has become as it were a part of our life of which we could not bear to be deprived. Hence we proclaim its reality in a judgment which is more than a judgment of cold fact, because it is in addition a glowing and heartfelt judgment of value. In a word, a religious value-judgment is a *personal conviction*, on which we stake all, and which we

[1] 2 Cor. v. 19.

hold because the influence of Christ upon us leaves us no option.

Not quite unnaturally objections were raised to this general view, some of them based on pure misunderstanding. Perhaps these objections are made less frequently now, for it has been noted that the British mind is accustomed to deal with novel theories in a fashion peculiarly its own. Presented with a new idea we are apt to say : " We never heard anything like this before " ; and for a time that is taken as final. Next we say : " It is contrary to the Bible." Eventually comes the murmur : " We knew it all the time." Something of the kind has occurred here. And yet even now it is occasionally said : Is not this theory of value-judgments in faith a new and elaborate plea that religious people may believe what they like, if only they like it very much ? Or may it not imply that in religion fancies are as good as facts, if only the fancies are comforting and inspiring ? Possibly this was a colourable charge as against certain ill-considered statements of the view I am discussing. Unwary phrases used at the start may have fostered the notion, not altogether inexcusable, that judgments of value were random wishes, which the believer made up out of his own head. But even if this were so, it no more invalidates the theory than initial defects in wireless apparatus touch the fact that to-day we in Britain can hear people speaking in America.

We have seen that the personal conviction of the religious man is a conviction about facts, and

CHARACTER OF RELIGIOUS KNOWLEDGE

is built on facts. It takes the fact of Christ, for example, and affirms its infinite worth for men. Now this is not affected by the undoubted circumstance that the conviction in question may have its origin in conscience or desire, and in that sense may be called subjective. The point is that the believing affirmation refers not to the inward experiences of the person making it—though it may and does spring out of such experiences—but to something real and objective, in this case the personality of Jesus. That reality is *there*, confronting us whether or not we attend to it, possessing its worth for men whether or not we feel it. There is an immeasurable difference between knowing *about* Christ and knowing Him as our personal Lord and Saviour. Purely theoretical knowledge on the subject of Christ does not of itself lead us into the fellowship of God; it is indeed quite compatible with our rejecting Him to His face. But to know Him as the Saviour who brings us to the Father is to have knowledge of a different kind. It is different in kind, but it is just as true, just as verifiable in suitable ways, just as closely in touch with reality as the other, and believing men would stare in amazement at the suggestion that Christ, or the God whom Christ reveals, was only a fancy in their minds. But this time it is knowledge suffused by personal faith, fed by faith and feeding it. It consists in a heartfelt response to revelation, precisely as our trustful knowledge of a friend is a response to all that he has done and been for us, to everything in him well fitted to win our confidence and love. The redeeming God is no more the fabrication of our dream than are those who love us in our homes; but in neither case is the knowledge we possess to be called *scientific* in character or origin.[1]

This analogy, the experience of friendship, is worth looking at closely; for, as I must think, it has received nothing like the prominence it deserves as a picture or paradigm of the birth of religious faith. A suspicious mind, bent on misinterpreting the simplest actions, is by that very fact cut off from genuine friendship; this man can never see into the other's heart. A cautious mind, apt to test every plank in the bridge before putting down his foot, comes to

---

[1] Why should it be assumed that if we are to know God, it must be through the kind of thinking the physicist indulges in for the four or five hours *per diem* he spends in his laboratory, and not rather through the kind of thinking (which in that region too can be sufficiently critical and unfriendly to delusion) which comes naturally to him all the rest of his waking day, among his family or friends? There is a good deal to be said for the view that contact with spiritual life must be made in appropriate ways. " The materialist," Eddington has said, ". who is convinced that all phenomena arise from electrons and quanta and the like controlled by mathematical formulæ, must presumably hold the belief that his wife is a rather elaborate differential equation; but he is probably tactful enough not to obtrude this opinion in domestic life. If this kind of scientific dissection is felt to be inadequate and irrelevant in ordinary personal relationships, it is surely out of place in the most personal relationship of all— that of the human soul to the Divine Spirit" (*The Nature of the Physical World*, p. 341).

friendship slowly. He waits and ponders and delays; then one day he looks into the other's eyes, and these two souls touch and know each other, and the friendship has begun. Previously he was like the rustic in an art gallery, standing before some great picture, seeing nothing but patches of paint on canvas; now he is like the same man after he has caught sight of the picture's meaning and opened his soul to take in its beauty. Just so, we may have been acquainted with the history of Jesus from our earliest years, while yet it has left us cold and unconcerned; then one day, by sudden change or as the outcome of a long preparatory process, the scales fall from your eyes, and it dawns upon us that in this Jesus God is finding us and we are finding Him. When now we say that we *know* Him, we mean that our whole being goes out to apprehend Him and to hold Him fast. Theology is built up out of such personal convictions. It consists of truths to which Christian men can bear witness. It is well to buttress the theological edifice with the best available scientific and philosophical argument; it is still better defensively to meet philosophy with philosophy, and thus to show those who may be kept from faith by philosophical objections that a deeper and more adequate philosophy will rob these objections of their force. These things are good, but they are not vital to the fundamental things of religion. Were they vital, men could have no right to their faith in God until they had found for it a metaphysical vindication.

THE CHRISTIAN APPREHENSION OF GOD

But it is not so. The simplest believer, kneeling in her cottage on the bare hillside, is as sure of God as the most learned theologian in the world.

It comes then to this, that the sympathetic and trustful insight which is a prerequisite of getting in touch with a person is not at all the same thing as purely intellectual perception. Scientific method will not bring us to intimate acquaintance with either God or man. We know the facts of the physical world in one way, those of the spiritual world in another. In both instances, however, we have real knowledge. Judgments of a simply logical kind, to which a simply logical certainty belongs, occur in the one case; judgments of trust, of conviction, of personal and kindling response to absolute values, occur in the other. If such inward convictions prove themselves valid every day in the profoundest experiences of friendship, there is no intrinsic reason why they should deceive us in the realm of spiritual faith.

Thus, when we a little stand off from the theory of value-judgments in religion and strive once more to estimate its meaning, two things at once become evident. First, it is far from being new. Instead of ranking as a modern invention, it can be traced back to Christ Himself. He said: " Every one that is of the truth hears my voice " ;[1] He also said, in words we cannot too deeply ponder: " If any man willeth to do the will of

[1] John xviii. 37.

CHARACTER OF RELIGIOUS KNOWLEDGE

my Father, he shall know of the doctrine."[1] In brief, our spiritual knowledge, unlike (say) mathematical perception, is morally conditioned. The man who does not care for goodness is not accidentally but necessarily blind in matters of faith. He does not see the friendship of God waiting to be taken; he cannot understand what such friendship could be for. Let us be quite frank with ourselves: the truth that God is love, that we may have the forgiveness of sins, that death cannot separate us from the Father, is not clear to everybody without exception, or to anybody at all times. Indeed, we all of us know perfectly that our inward persuasion of such things moves up and down through various degrees of certainty according to the moral plane on which we are living. The same principle, that spiritual knowledge has moral conditions, is expressed by St Paul when he writes that "the natural man receiveth not the things of the Spirit, for they are foolishness to him; neither can he know them, for they are spiritually discerned."[2] Truths of the Spirit of God, that is, are sheer folly to one who does not read them with a spiritual eye. Thus the view—of which the theory of religious value-judgments is only a technical elaboration—that there is no true knowledge of God which does not come through faith, and that faith, while a Divine gift, is also a morally qualified human attitude, is as old as Christianity.

And secondly, it is a principle on which the

[1] John vii. 17. [2] 1 Cor. ii. 14.

preacher or evangelist goes by instinct. Such an advocate of Christ makes appeal, not to the scientific intelligence of his hearers, but (to use the old good word) to their *souls*; *i.e.* to their complete nature in its most personal aspect. When men are converted, it is not because they have been overwhelmed by irrefutable argument, but because they have been subjected to an irresistible impression; and in the great majority of instances the impression has been made specifically on the conscience. By that inward witness the authority of the heard message is recognized and owned. The God who speaks in conscience is one with the God who confronts us in Jesus. Christ and conscience—these are the great factors which lead men into the obedience and the fellowship of God. Thus once more, by the natural procedure of the evangelist, the distinction between scientific and religious knowledge is confirmed.

This is perhaps the point at which to introduce one matter of importance. The value-judgments of religion, or, in better words, the personal convictions of faith, must not be regarded as simple postulates. In strictness, a postulate is a belief of a quite definite kind. It is a belief we have resolved to cling to because of its indispensable value to our inner life. We *must* retain it, we feel, otherwise the badness of the world would be insufferable and we should prefer to cease living and go out in nothingness. We assert something, that is, as true on the ground of our intense and

CHARACTER OF RELIGIOUS KNOWLEDGE

ineradicable desire that it should be true. Now it cannot be too emphatically said that Christian doctrines are not postulates in this sense—not at least doctrines which form a genuine part of Christianity. They are not postulates, because they have been generated in the mind and heart of man by the self-revelation of God. His self-disclosure, His awakening and arresting Word, has been the producing cause of these convictions; it is because God has shown us that in character He is such and such that we are sure of this or that. The Christian faith in immortality, for instance, is not merely a passionate human cry for another life; it has been evoked, rather, by God's unveiling Himself to men as faithfully and unchangeably Redeemer, and thereby conveying to them the assurance that He will not leave them in the dust or permit death to make a difference to the bond that unites them to Him. It is therefore simply mistaken to suppose that in affirming the personality or the love of God we are doing nothing more than argue, wistfully and pathetically, from the presence of a yearning in man's heart to the reality of the object yearned for. There is no need to deny the inferential value of such desires, if they are profound enough, persistent enough, closely enough bound up with the foundations of our moral nature. But even so, it must still be said that it is not merely on such desires that the great Christian convictions rest. We believe what as Christians we do believe for the reason that God has come personally to seek us, and in Jesus Christ has offered us communion with Himself.

Up to this point I have been accentuating the special character of religious knowledge. Let us formulate its distinctiveness once more, borrowing for the purpose a description of the two chief sorts of knowledge. " There is, first of all, the matter-of-fact knowledge of the world around us, which comes to its perfection in the matter of thoroughness and exactitude in the natural sciences. There is, secondly, the practical acquaintance or familiarity gained by experience and aided by sympathetic intuition and appreciation, such acquaintance as is well exemplified in the relation of friends to one another. Scientific knowledge aims at being severely intellectual, impersonal, and unemotional. But the intimate knowledge which friends have one of another is not the result of a process of reasoning or scientific research, but is based on mutual confidence and affection gained through practical experience and insight."[1] Faith in God is analogous to trust in a great and noble friend. But now that this important distinction has been made, it is time for the complementary truth that nothing which has been said above points to, or advocates, an ultimate and irreconcilable dualism in knowledge. It is one thing to hold that science and faith issue from, and appeal to, different mental interests; it is quite another thing, and surely quite misleading, to hold that

[1] Miall Edwards, *Philosophy of Religion*, p. 210.

CHARACTER OF RELIGIOUS KNOWLEDGE

science and faith have nothing to do with each other, or, even worse, must permanently remain in relations of hostility. No man who believes that his intelligence is a gift of God will ever consent to keep his scientific knowledge and his religious knowledge in separate and hermetically sealed compartments, with no communication or mutual influence between. As it has been put : " Thought refuses to be confined by artificial boundaries. The Christian who thinks cannot keep God in his soul and leave Him out of his world."[1]

Yet the attempt has often been made to do just this. And it was the suspicion that certain Ritschlian thinkers, in their youthful and less considered statements, were once more endeavouring to do this very thing that gave its edge to some of the most telling criticisms directed against them. In an early pamphlet, written over fifty years ago, Herrmann of Marburg declared that a man might quite well be a materialist in philosophy and a Christian in religious faith. Twenty years later as a student I happened in the course of a country walk to quote to him that startling opinion, and I ventured (I hope with respect) to ask whether he still adhered to it. His reply was to pour scorn on it as indefensible. Whether or not he described it as " a sin of his youth " I cannot now recall; but manifestly he regarded it as something to be disowned and forgotten as belonging to an outworn phase of thought. Incidentally, his attitude read a lesson to all who

[1] Sorley, *Moral Values and the Idea of God*, p. 479.

are much more anxious to demonstrate their own undeviating intellectual consistency than to appear as seekers after truth.

It is vain, then, to revive the late scholastic dictum that a proposition may be false in theology but true in philosophy. This is to violate what may be called the honour of the mind, and it unfailingly brings its revenge. Faith that every truth, when scanned from the ultimate point of view, is in harmony with all the rest of truth is part of faith in God Himself, who will not put us intellectually to confusion. Nothing that science has *proved* can be doubtful for the believer who keeps his windows open toward the light. This is not a point of theory merely, or we might be content to argue it academically; it is a vital concern of personal religion. It is the *same* world which we contemplate now from the standpoint of scientific interpretation, now from that of believing trust. We could not serve God as He bids us serve Him in the actual universe except as in some degree we are able to understand the course of events and to reckon on the steadfast constitution of things. We can only do our daily work, for example—and for the building of character there is nothing to compare with work—if to an appreciable extent we know how things behave under varied conditions; and to know how things behave, with some exactness, is science. Hence the two mental attitudes, the scientific and the religious, demand each other; and one task of theology will always be to show, by every sound

CHARACTER OF RELIGIOUS KNOWLEDGE

form of argument, that the real conclusions of scientific inquiry and the basal Christian certainties, so far from being at variance, are complementary to one another and are both needed for even an approximately satisfying view of the universe as a whole. The preacher never shows to less advantage than when he is trying to ridicule scientific research, and (in spite of great leaders in that field who are also humble and reverent disciples of Christ) leaving on the listener's mind the impression that those who are toiling in laboratory and study, often for little earthly reward, are most probably secret atheists and in any case enemies of the human race. When we or our children are sick, we eagerly claim the aid of scientific medicine, and thank God for it. Shall we not own with grateful reverence all that the researchers are doing for the relief of human pain and the ennobling of life by the improvement of its worst conditions ? Whichcote's aphorism could hardly be improved upon : " Nothing is worse done than what is ill done for religion ; that must not be done in defence of religion which is contrary to religion."

It is our duty, therefore, to believe in and unflinchingly work for the unity of all we know. Yet such unity is hard to reach. The tension between science and faith to-day is acute, as it always has been ; as we may be fairly certain it will be to the end. Some people think this a great pity ; but is that so clear ? Faith is never easy, and we are called upon to fight the good fight in

THE CHRISTIAN APPREHENSION OF GOD

the domain of thought as truly as in that of practice. Here also we have to endure to the end and thus, in Christ's words, win our souls.

One thing at all events is worth saying. In the heat and toil of the struggle, we may well beware of specious short-cuts to the reconciliation of science and faith. One of these short-cuts is the contention that the two disparate kinds of knowledge have no mutual relationships whatever; but on this we need not pause again. We have only one mind, which cannot permanently be divided against itself. Another is the argument that religious problems could all be solved quite simply and expeditiously if only we had the courage to treat them by strictly scientific methods, if we reasoned about God and salvation pretty much as we do about radium or protozoa. This hardy suggestion crops up at intervals, apparently without the faintest consciousness on the part of its champions that it has often been tried and is invariably found to lead nowhere.

The foregoing pages make it at least highly probable that scientific methods and the methods of religious faith—as of human friendship—are not the same. Let all possible scientific questions be solved, even by perfectly lucid and consistent answers, and still the real problems of faith would not have been touched. We should not be one step-nearer a reply to the vital religious question: How can I, finite and guilty man, have fellowship with God? The enabling grace of God, the freedom of man's will—these are not matters to

CHARACTER OF RELIGIOUS KNOWLEDGE

be treated of in the physiological laboratory or by the method of statistics. If spirit were a material phenomenon, if the objects of faith were spatial, something doubtless might be said for the policy of tracing natural law in the spiritual world; for the application, as it is put technically, of physical or biological categories to the experiences of the religious man. The true task of reflective faith, rather, is to search for spiritual law in the natural world, for all real explanation consists in rendering the lower fact intelligible in the light of the higher. Or, to put it more comprehensively, what we are summoned to do is so to interpret the realities of history and of Nature by selective insight as to catch the message they bring us from the self-revealing God.

CHAPTER III

THE IDEA OF REVELATION

In the last chapter an attempt was made to set forth what claimed to be sound positions regarding the nature of religious knowledge, the ways in which we come to possess it, and the methods of proof or verification which are appropriate to the case. Now we turn to the correlative subject—not, this time, our believing knowledge, but the reality we know, or revelation. And let us not forget at any stage of the discussion that revelation, which taken by itself is only an abstract noun, really stands for the most concrete and personal object with which we can have to do, viz., God, as He makes Himself known savingly to man. If this be overlooked, the debate over revelation may easily become as cold and lifeless as a treatise on symbolic logic.

The convictions of faith, as we have seen, do not create themselves. They are not the product of hard speculative thinking, nor are they shadowy emanations of a dreamer's brain. On the contrary, like every form of knowledge, faith is a response to a reality which evokes, invites, and rewards acquaintance. The revealed fact is not man-made or poetically contrived; it is *given* or presented or found to be inescapably *there;* it confronts the human mind not in the same fashion but just as positively as Nature confronts the scientist, or historical events confront the historian. What mediates revelation in its highest form is a significant fact or series of facts occurring in time, " fact " being used here in a sense capacious enough to include personality ; and the task of faith is to discern and receive and proclaim the redemptive meaning which these facts contain for the sinful. All religious knowledge of God, wherever existing, comes by revelation ; otherwise we should be committed to the incredible position that man can know God without His willing to be known. In modern discussions, the older distinction between natural and revealed religion is tending to recede into the background, and a new distinction is taking its place. Thoughtful men are now disposed to differentiate, rather, between the knowledge of God obtained through external Nature on the one hand, and on the other that obtained through the moral and spiritual life of man. All higher knowledge of God, indeed, comes through moral and religious experience.

Let us approach the subject by first asking: What are the great thoughts of the Bible on revelation, as well as on the conditions under which it is received ?

It is obvious, to begin with, that the Bible makes no effort whatever to *argue*, in the philosophical manner, either that God exists, or that He can be known. The immediate certainty of union and communion with God is the starting-point of all Biblical writers. Their assurance that God is real was no drawn-out inference ; it was a direct intuition. Proof that there is a God, and that He concerns Himself with man, belong to apologetics or to a certain form of evangelism, not to the spontaneous utterance of faith. Some great problems settle themselves for the prophetic mind, not because they have been solved by reasoning, but by the prophet being lifted to such a height that for him they disappear. The eagle flying through the sky is not troubled how to cross the rivers.

God, then, both exists and is known. How has this knowledge come about? To that question the answer of Scripture is clear and uncompromising: He is known by revelation, and only so. As it is put with deep simplicity by A. B. Davidson: "If men know God, it is because He has made Himself known to them. The idea of man reaching to knowledge or fellowship of God through his own efforts is foreign to the Old Testament. . . . God brings Himself near to men. . . . Moses and the prophets are nowhere represented as thoughtful minds reflecting on the Unseen and ascending to elevated conceptions of Godhead: the Unseen manifests itself to them, and they know it."[1] The prophets in every case are men to whom God spoke first, and they answered His call. That the conviction of God, and His urgent claim on them, does not rise out of their own speculative ponderings, or from any self-induced rapture, is sufficiently demonstrated by the fact that the greater prophets shrink from

[1] Hastings' *Dictionary of the Bible*, Vol. II, p. 197.

the realization of the Divine presence; His communication is a burden to them, from which in their painfully felt inadequacy and unworthiness they at first are tempted to escape. A higher hand has been laid on them, constraining them to listen, and, when they have listened, to obey. The same emphasis on the revealing initiative of God comes out in a memorable phrase of St Paul. " Now that you have come to know God," he writes to the Galatians; then he checks himself, and adds, " or rather, now that you are known of God."[1] God is on the ground first and takes the first step. As Keble somewhere puts it:

> Get up as early as you may,
> Grace, like an angel, runs before.

It is assumed here, manifestly, that there can be men of the prophetic spirit, who have been given power to see into the life of things with a more piercing view than the great mass of their fellows. No one, at all events no one with any understanding of life's deeper issues, will deny that there is such a thing as vicarious suffering, from which untold benefit accrues to others; nor can I see why, in parallel fashion, there should not be such a thing as vicarious insight. We certainly could not, any of us, have written Keats' *Ode on a Grecian Urn*, or Wordsworth's *Lines Composed above Tintern Abbey;* but we can appreciate them once they have been created for us by poetic genius; we can in some measure

[1] Gal. iv. 9.

follow the movements of the poet's imagination, with the sense that we are being enriched with a beauty and truth that time cannot wither. In the same way, we could not have originated Hosea's ineffably tender vision of the love of God, or the ideal of the Divinely redemptive Sufferer pictured in the 53rd chapter of Isaiah; but we can drink the great thoughts there enshrined, and find life and peace in the disclosure of God's mind they convey. The prophets of Israel, if any in the world's history can be so described, are supernaturally inspired men, bringing truth on which ever since the world has lived and will always live; but they are not morbid or unnatural. They are so far—for it is only " so far " that any analogy to the prophets can be found—in line with acknowledged facts of new spiritual creativeness in other fields. But the emotional and intuitional enlightenment from above that makes a man a prophet is higher by far than inspiration in any other form; for in his words an absolute authority speaks, and he is enabled so to declare God as to bring men into fellowship with the Eternal.

Let us now turn to the question, what are the leading ideas concerning revelation which a reader of the Bible, if sufficiently observant, might gather out of its pages. As a preliminary remark, governing all the rest of what is said here, let it be emphasized as a fact now tolerably well known that the Bible does not encourage us to think of revelation as taking place by the sudden or preternatural conveyance of mere information or

THE IDEA OF REVELATION

bare doctrinal theorems. It rather bids us conceive of God as unveiling His character and purpose through objective events and historical personalities, which faith is taught to interpret as luminous with transcendent meaning and predictive of yet greater Divine manifestations in the future.

The Bible depicts revelation, in this sense, as taking place in two manners or stages. One stage is primary, the other remedial.

Into the primary revelation three factors enter. Of these three, the first is Nature. "The heavens declare the glory of God, and the firmament showeth his handywork";[1] and the revelation thus given is unceasing and universal. The kindness of the Father, Jesus said, is seen in His making the sun to rise on the evil and the good.[2] According to St Paul, God left not Himself without witness, in that He did good, and gave rain from heaven and fruitful seasons.[3] The second factor is history. In a later speech at Athens, St Paul points to the guidance and sovereign control of nations as a continuous indication of God.[4] And the third factor is the moral consciousness of man, with its intimations of a Higher Will—that inward eye, of which Jesus said that, if it be single, the whole body will be full of light.[5]

This primary revelation, with these three elements or constituents of Nature, history, and conscience, furnishes in the view of Scripture all

[1] Ps. xix. 1. [2] Matt. v. 45. [3] Acts xiv. 17.
[4] Acts xvii. 26-27. [5] Matt. vi. 22.

the conditions for the rise and progress of true religion. But the outcome, when there is a positive outcome, should not be called "Natural Religion," as if it had grown up of itself, in untended and unenriched soil. Like religion of every kind, it has been called into being by revelation.

None the less, from an examination of the actual human world, St Paul draws the melancholy conclusion that this primary revelation has failed. Neither Nature nor history has made on man a sufficiently deep impression. Even conscience has proved unavailing; for, as the Apostle declares, uncontrolled sensuality renders men at last incapable of recognizing the imperatives of God within the soul.[1] Not that the longing for God is thereby quenched. That is something which can never be extinguished, and its ineradicable character is evinced by what the Apostle considers to be the vain attempts of idolatrous heathenism to make a religion for itself.

According to the Bible, this dark situation could only be retrieved by a new and better self-manifestation of God, so powerful and tenacious in its effects that sin must give way, and eventually be driven vanquished from the field. This, the revelation of God *par excellence*, takes shape century after century in great historical incidents and persons, through which and through whom shines the light that saves.

These historical acts and persons, in the Biblical

[1] Rom. i.-ii.

THE IDEA OF REVELATION

view, display themselves within a specific area or sphere of human life, namely, the history of Israel; and they are interpreted to Israel, age after age, by prophetic men. It is possible, I think, to discern an important difference between the first kind of revelation and the second. The first is pictured as given to all men; the starry heavens above and the moral law within, to anticipate Kant's famous words, are perceptible by all, without exception, and in both God speaks. But the second, just because it is God's intention to work it out through the medium of human personal influence, begins necessarily at one centre and spreads outward from that nucleus. Here, we may interject, one aspect of the Biblical thought of election comes out—it is election, not to monopoly, but to appointed service.[1] The experience of redemption took at the outset a particularized form, and was universalized only gradually; God spoke, throughout Israel's history, in sundry times and divers manners, until the fullness of the times came, and He spoke to the whole world by His Son.

Prophecy is an unfailing element in the Biblical idea of revelation, noticeably in its Old Testament stage. In the second half of Isaiah, for example, strong emphasis is laid on the fact that prophecy is a token of God's revealing and redemptive activity. It is excessively difficult to tell what went on in prophetic minds, but we can see clearly enough they were filled with the conviction that God had touched them imperiously and

[1] On this point, see Chapter VIII.

uttered His will in such a way that they knew the voice to be His. Their experience, by the nature of the case, was not such that we can analyze it scientifically. Prophets were to Israel what, in God's purpose, Israel was to be to the whole world. At critical epochs in the nation's life, they came forward to decipher the signs of the times, and to translate the meaning of events into language intelligible to their contemporaries; for, as has been said, "revelation is no revelation until it takes the shape of human thought."

Here two important points call for attention. In the first place, let us carefully observe that, according to the teaching of Scripture, God's revelation of Himself, though relative, is true. It is of course relative to the Divinely-evoked capacities of the human mind. To-day men are fond of the notion that real apprehension of God is impossible for minds like ours, because, from the intrinsic make of our faculties, we cannot form ideas about Divine things except as we falsify them in the very act. Without discussing the philosophical soundness of this, we may at all events lay down that Scripture knows nothing of such an idea. Biblical writers, though well aware that God dwells "in light that none can approach," could not have formed the idea that God, as self-revealed to men, is not God as He is in Himself. There is, as has been pointed out, no suggestion in Scripture that His revelation of Himself "is meant merely to be regulative of human life, while what He is in truth remains

THE IDEA OF REVELATION

far away in a transcendental background, out of which it is impossible for it to advance, and into which it is impossible for man to penetrate."[1] Yet, while teaching that God can be known, and in Christ is known, the Bible can also say that He is unknowable, *i.e.* unfathomable. That is the tenor of St Paul's adoring apostrophe: "O the depth of the riches both of the wisdom and knowledge of God! How unsearchable are his judgments, and his ways past finding out."[2] In such an ejaculation, born of religious feeling, the contradictories are held together firmly, that God is known and yet is not known. In experience the difficulty does not vanish, but it becomes endurable because it is seen to be necessary. In Christ, God is known as He actually is, yet in Him even so there remain regions unknown, which faith can never exhaust. It is the same vital, not accidental, antinomy as we meet with in the familiar words: "To know the love of Christ, which passeth knowledge."[3]

And secondly, in view of the historical development of revelation, of which the Bible is the record, a distinction must of course be made between the less and more perfect degrees in which the Divine reality, thus being gradually disclosed, was apprehended by the human mind. There are the two facts, and neither must be used to cancel the other, namely, the Light shining through into the receiving mind, and the only

[1] A. B. Davidson, *ut supra*.   [2] Rom. xi. 33.
[3] Eph. iii. 19.

THE CHRISTIAN APPREHENSION OF GOD

partial transparency of the medium. So there may be a genuine revelation to a prophet who yet may not understand all that God is trying to say to him. Nay more; he may actually distort and darken the traversing rays, so as to leave on those to whom he speaks a misleading impression of this or that feature in the character of the God he is proclaiming. If I read in the New Testament the words, " God is love," and recognize them as a description of the Father immediately reflected in Jesus Christ, I inevitably am disconcerted by certain pictures of God presented in the Old Testament. In the 63rd chapter of Isaiah, for example, these words are put on the lips of Jahveh: " I trod the peoples in mine anger, and trampled them in my fury; and their life-blood is sprinkled on my garments ";[1] but faith tells me these descriptions cannot both be true exactly as they stand. Had the prophet known Jesus Christ, he would still presumably have had something to say about the wrath of God, which is a great fact; but he would have said it otherwise. What exactly are the elements in the Old Testament which have to be discarded by the Christian, because in Christ he has found the full and perfect truth, is much too large a question to be debated here. But that such elements exist is undeniable; they follow simply from the fact that God revealed Himself by degrees in history, as men were able to bear it. Christ Himself drew attention to the imperfect acquaintance with the will of God

[1] Isa. lxiii. 3.

THE IDEA OF REVELATION

possessed in earlier times, and for us it is enough to accept His judgment.

Whatever the defects of the human medium, none the less the Light shone through, more and more, until in Jesus the medium, as faith has always confessed, became utterly and stainlessly transparent. And the record deposited by that rising and broadening self-disclosure of God is the Bible. We do well to take as our own the words of the great Biblical scholar, Robertson Smith, for as a statement of truth they could hardly be improved upon: " If I am asked why I receive Scripture as the Word of God, and as the only perfect rule of faith and life, I answer with all the fathers of the Protestant Church: Because the Bible is the only record of the redeeming love of God, because in the Bible alone I find God drawing near to man in Christ Jesus, and declaring to us in Him His will for our salvation. And this record I know to be true by the witness of His Spirit in my heart, whereby I am assured that none other than God Himself is able to speak such words to my soul."

When we pass from Scripture into the regions of theology as it developed through the centuries, we launch out on a difficult and uncharted sea of opinion. Men's ideas of revelation and of faith always vary together; and as in early Christian times faith took on a strongly intellectualistic cast, and came more and more to stand for acceptance of the orthodox creed, the idea of revelation sank along with it. It was thought of very much as a theoretic communication addressed to the human understanding; or as numerous pieces of information about God. At last came the religious upheaval of the Reformation. Faith regained its experimental character, and hence revelation also was looked at from a fresh point of view. Not that the Reformers set forth an elaborated theory of the matter; it would be truer to say that in a great wave of religious life and insight they forced their way back to the New Testament, grasped the meaning of Christ for sinful men, and settled by something like unerring intuition one or two crucial questions which were only theorized at a later stage.

One nineteenth century thinker who two generations since helped many people to clear insight on these matters was Rothe. The problem discussed by him in an essay which in its day was famous may be stated thus: Is revelation essentially outward or inward, or both equally? His solution was gained by way of a fruitful distinction. On the one side, he argues, stands the interposition of God in the actual history of the world, and this he calls *Manifestation*. On the other side is the Divine enlightenment of prophetic men, enabling them to interpret the events in which God is manifested; and to this he gives the name *Inspiration*. Both things together, outward event and insight quickened from above, form, as a living unity, revelation. It is perhaps an unsatisfactory feature of this view that the

THE IDEA OF REVELATION

manifestation of God is confined to external events, whether of Nature or history. There can be nothing but approval for Rothe's wish to bring out the essentially historical form of revelation; but in history there is far more than outward incident. Surely, for example, our Lord's experience of Sonship is the highest revelation of God's Fatherhood; yet that experience of His is no outward event. None the less, Rothe was completely justified in emphasizing the point that events, simply as bare happenings in space and time, can never of themselves suffice to make God known to man; beside them, vitally connected or correlated with them, must go the prophetic insight which exhibits the events as charged with Divine significance. What we behold in the New Testament, and what, as we see it there, acts upon us as a disclosure of God's holy love, is not merely the career of Jesus; it is this career evoking and satisfying the faith of the disciples, and inspiring them to a unique type of believing witness.

Ever since Rothe, theology has kept fast hold of his fertile principle that revelation meets us pre-eminently in the field of history. It is history that has made human life what it is, and it is in history that God has approached man, to make clear His gracious mind. In bringing this out, there is no need to confine revelation to the person of Jesus, as some recent thinkers have been apt to do; nor, again, is it wise to isolate Jesus from the conditions of age and country amid which His Divine personality unfolded through life, up to the Cross. While, however, if He is to guide us to the Father, Jesus must be seen and known in His habit as He lived, nothing must be allowed to divert our minds again from the truth that, although not the only medium of revelation, He is the supreme and final medium. In this context we cannot lay too much stress on personality, as the one possible mirror of God, if we are to make Christian religion intelligible to an age which rightly regards personality as the highest product of time—a fact transcendent, creative, irreducible to simpler elements, and therefore, if indwelt by God, the fit organ of His self-unveiling.

Furthermore, when we take it so, it transpires that the revelation which calls forth saving faith and imparts to such faith not probability merely, but certainty and triumphant power—the person of Jesus Christ, in short—is something that historical science cannot touch, much less destroy. Let the man whom a hunger for goodness has driven to seek God come face to face with Christ as presented in the New Testament; let him submit himself to the impression Christ makes, humbling him to the very dust by holiness, forgiving and lifting him up to new hope and courage by love; and the reality of God as his Saviour will come home to him. His heart will open through Christ to faith in the Father. We apprehend God in Christ with certainty because, as St Paul puts it, He apprehends us. The New Testament picture of Jesus, entering the receptive heart, needs no certificate of truth ; like the sun, it shines by its own light and attests itself ; it forces upon us the moral decision whether we *dare* reject it as only the fabrication of devout fancy, the imagined construction of minds as blind and guilty as our own. That is light by which we see, and that is revelation which actually brings us into pardoned fellowship with God ; but in neither case can there be any proof other than the fact itself. Here, indeed, is the initial fixed point apart from which the Christian religion cannot make a beginning : unless Jesus renders His own reality evident by His power to lead us to God, unless what He is shines through what He does, the preacher or evangelist is powerless. He cannot by any eloquence of argument make men feel that Christ means God ; but he knows that if, in the Spirit's power, he can show Christ to men, the picture will vindicate itself. It furnishes indeed a sure ground of faith unaffected by the numberless questions that historical criticism may and must raise concerning the Gospel narratives. Again, just because the supreme revelation meets us in Jesus, it wins the spontaneous assent of the free and conscious spirit ; it is not imposed by any legal or external compulsion. For the presence of God in Christ, when felt at all, bears in upon us as an overpowering and irresistible fact. Faith, called into being by what we see in Christ, is a faith not manufactured for us by man, or thrust on us by public opinion ; it is *given* us by God through His self-presentation in Jesus, very much as confidence is given to fighting men by the presence among them of a born leader. To ask for proof that what shines to us through Christ is God, is like asking for proof that luminous objects are visible. The Christian whom Christ has led into communion with the Father is merely giving Christ His right name when he calls Him, in an unshared sense, the Revealer.

Before embarking on a closer study of revelation as thus perfected in Christ, it may be useful to glance briefly at the bearing of our topic on the work of the foreign missionary. Or, to be more precise, on the work of the missionary among primitive peoples. Warneck tells us that primitive animistic races regard the Gospel as a quite novel thing, viz., a religion claiming to be revealed. No such claim is made by their own worships. "None of the religions of the Indian Archipelago or of Africa," he writes, "has ever dreamt of a Divine self-manifestation to men." For them, the one source of religious knowledge is tradition—what they learn from the old men of the tribe, not from God. And to this he adds the striking remark, that of the missionary's hearers none ever shows an inclination to dispute the claim of Christianity to be revealed. "During my evangelistic work," he states, "never once has a heathen asked me how he was to know that my message was true, and was from God." The truth is felt to be its own witness. Thus it would appear that the primitive mind is made for revelation—predisposed to acknowledge it even when not yielding it practical obedience, and unsatisfied till confronted with it. Just at the point where the Christian can offer no coercive proof, none is sought for. From all this Warneck concludes that no one need hope to touch and win such races who does not himself hold that in Christ we have a true revelation of God, or who does not proclaim the Gospel as a message concerning redemptive deeds of God which is certain, when proclaimed, to commend itself to conscience and heart. Only so will he be recognized by animistic peoples as bringing them more than already they possess. In the absence of this, he is convinced, they will indubitably fall away to Mohammedanism, which does claim to be a revealed faith, and thus wields a weapon against which no lower worship can make a stand.

The general idea of Revelation, though difficult to define precisely, may perhaps be taken as signifying such a disclosure of God as in any degree meets and satisfies the religious need. For religion, that and that only is revelation which enables us to apprehend God through the medium of His working in human lives and in the world. But even within the religious field we draw a still narrower circle. We specially reserve the word to indicate, as it has been put, " those creative acts or events or personalities, through the instrumentality of which a new type of religious experience, of fellowship with God, is initiated and given its specific character."

But these are generalities. The real point, after all, is the Christian claim that a perfect and final revelation of God, in the sense described, has been imparted through and in Jesus Christ. In Him we see, once and for ever, what God would have us know concerning Himself as the Judge and Redeemer of us all; and the liberating and cleansing effect of Christ upon our lives is guarantee to faith that the revelation which He embodies is true. That which in fact does bring us to the Father, does persuade us to adhere to God as holy love, is His self-revelation. But if so, then what we learn of God by looking at Jesus is, or ought to be, determinative of *all* our religious beliefs. What He was and did and taught and experienced, as exhibited by the witness of the New Testament, is our key to God's purpose and nature; for, as Hort once said, " belief in Christ is not a supplement to belief in God, but the only true foundation of it." The man who really understands this, and lets it rule his theological thinking, is in principle delivered from the haunting temptation to conceive revelation as a complex of supernaturally communicated doctrines. He now takes seriously the great declaration of the Epistle to the Hebrews that " God has spoken to us in a Son."[1] In practice most people discover that the best way to prevent the term " revelation " from sinking, as it may do so easily, into something cold, impersonal, and didactic is to set at its heart the Cross and Resurrection of

[1] Heb. i. 2.

our Lord. It is supremely a great deed, a drama in two chapters, that shows what God is—it is Christ's death for the sinful and His triumph over death in their name. Our faith stands upon the entire fact of Christ; but the fact of Christ is truncated if we stop short at the Cross and leave the Resurrection out. Had Christ's story terminated at the grave, our thought of God would be other to-day than it actually is; for a Christ whom we know to have been raised by the Father, and a Christ of whom we do not know whether He was raised or not, are quite different beings. As different, they convey different impressions of God and, as a consequence, they evoke different types of faith.

The foregoing contention may now be summarized in the statement that in the faithful mirror of Christ, His personality and experience, we behold God. There can be no repealing of that great word: " He that hath seen me hath seen the Father."[1] And, as has been said memorably, " If God is like Jesus, the world has reason to be glad." In no other way could a God whom we should call " Father " be unveiled. If revelation is to be more than a bare verbal announcement, or a series of such announcements, it must come through a convincing portrait of God caught in and reflected by an infinitely good and loving spirit, in whose depths men might perceive and love it.

In view of this, we may venture to enumerate

[1] John xiv. 9.

THE CHRISTIAN APPREHENSION OF GOD

as follows the chief constitutive features of revelation, as not exemplified merely but consummated in Christ. They appear to be five in number:

(1) Revelation is personal. It comes from the living God, it is mediated at its highest point through Jesus, it claims and appeals to man in his whole personality. In a word, it is from God through Christ to man. We may best compare it not so much to our efforts to become acquainted with a great man as to his taking steps to seek us out and offer us his friendship.

(2) Revelation in quality is moral. It attests itself freely to conscience and feeling; the testimony of our higher nature is on its side and wins for it spontaneous recognition. The deepest law of personality would be outraged by any alleged revelation which confronted us as a body of statutory dogma, imposing itself externally, and dictating a message to which the recipient brings only a passive acquiescence. Legalism of that kind, at this crucial point, would prove a new burden to conscience, not its relief, still less its inspiration. The loftier the nature of a friend, the more it is felt that to yield to his influence is one and the same thing with the exertion of moral freedom; yet no human friend evokes as Christ does that unreserved submission which is one with perfect liberty.

(3) Revelation is supernatural. Or, to put it otherwise, it is something which neither Nature

nor humanity, viewed in their normal character, can in the least explain ; something, rather, which is due to the creative action of God. The communion of God with man is definitely supernatural in the sense that it is traceable to His sovereign interposition within human experience in ways not necessitated, at any given moment, by the previous phase of the finite universe ; and the supernatural character of such interposition at varied times is sealed to us once for all by the conclusive personality of Christ, in whom God Himself comes as Redeemer. If we know God, it is not because men have found the way to Him, but because He has travelled the way to man. Revelation is God speaking ; our part is to hear and trustfully obey. The Word of God, His revealing utterance, is not to be argued with but something we have to listen to on our knees. By calling revelation supernatural it is not in the least meant that natural media are dispensed with, or that what are called the laws of Nature have been broken. What is meant is that in the events or persons we describe as revealing there is a peculiar and commanding presence of God, and in them He is working out a glorious purpose of love.

(4) Revelation is historical. It is in terms of historical reality that the grace of God is put within our reach. And this, if taken seriously, means that everything mechanical or magical drops away. Revelation does not reach the world

like a bullet out of a pistol ; at each stage the new self-disclosure of God serves itself heir to what went before, and bears it all up to a higher level. By a new living impulse it perpetuates and enhances what God has previously made known. Jesus fed His soul on the great words of the Old Testament. Emphasis on history implies, further, that the new insight is not reached by the pathway of abstract speculation. The faith that God is Holy Love broke on the human mind not through philosophic argument carried up to an undeniable conclusion, but through a certain Person having lived and died in this world. Of course in calling revelation historical, there can be no thought of limiting its significance or validity to a special epoch. The Gospel has no date but is above the power of time.

(5) Revelation evokes and nourishes faith. It calls out believing trust in human minds, and the trust thus initiated it is able more and more to deepen and enrich. It cannot be too emphatically said that what faith does is not to *create* the revelation it apprehends, but to *perceive* and accept it. The creative activity is on God's side ; on ours the attitude of faith, invariably, is that indicated by the Psalmist's words : " I will hear what God the Lord will speak."[1] Once God has spoken out His mind to men, the implications of His utterance are inexhaustible. In Christ there will always be more by far than we can take in.

[1] Ps. lxxxv. 8.

THE IDEA OF REVELATION

It is of first-rate importance that we should thus build from the start on the self-revelation of God in Christ, and that in consequence our thoughts of God should be regulated by Christ from end to end. Nothing in the theology of past centuries has done so much harm as the refusal, often unconscious, to be whole-hearted and thorough-going in acceptance of the real charter of Christian thinking about the Eternal : " He that hath seen me hath seen the Father." Too often men have said in effect : We believe that God resembles Christ, at least to a certain extent. Thereupon they proceeded to add various qualifications and reservations derived from non-Christian sources, such as pagan philosophy or religious beliefs in very doubtful keeping with the Spirit of Christ. And the consequence more than once has been that the all-decisive insight—stressed with such power by Luther—that God must be conceived wholly according to Christ, has been lost all over again. The one safeguard against these dangers is to draw our constitutive materials for the Christian conception of God from the only source which is perfectly pure. At each point Christ must be our guide. Let Him explain Himself ; do not obscure or modify His revelation by principles gathered elsewhere. Above all, never dilute His Gospel to the prescription of any half-religious philosophy.

But true as this is, and vitally important as it will always be to bring out the sufficiency and self-explaining character of the revelation in Christ, this is not to say that God has revealed Himself nowhere else. Neglect of this truth is certain to make trouble. Anyone who moves from the sound position that in Christ supremely and decisively we see God to the quite different position that revelation comes *exclusively* through Christ, has some very formidable questions to meet. Does not God influence men in other ways? Is there not in men a conscience through which He speaks, and is it not to conscience that the wise advocate of the Gospel fastens his appeal? If we deny this, do we not block the way for many who are seeking God; yes, and even the way to Christ Himself? In short, it is a mistaken conception of the dignity of the Christian religion which in some minds prompts a disparagement of other faiths, as if its honour were compromised by the admission of their value. As a witty French writer has put it, God has no need to grudge even His enemies their virtues. How far, then, is it true to assert a revelation of God outside the range of Christianity?

(1) There is the preparatory revelation of the Old Testament. This our Lord assumed as real and profound. Indeed, there is no New Testament conviction which may not be read as the completed form of Old Testament beginnings. To become Christians, the apostles had no need to renounce their former prophetic faith; and in this respect, at least preponderantly, they differed widely from Gentile converts. True, as the last chapter of St

THE IDEA OF REVELATION

Luke's Gospel more than suggests, it is only because we read the Old Testament with Christian eyes that we perceive its Christ-ward trend; but it is just the fact that it *can* be so read that gives the Old Testament a distinctive character. Things like the ethical monotheism of the prophets occur nowhere except on the line which, when prolonged, terminates in Jesus. The revealing work of God in Old Testament times is perhaps most conspicuous of all in the fact that the earlier dispensation pointed beyond itself, and, for the satisfaction of the ideals it had brought to birth, demanded a fulfilment which may truly be called infinite. In other words, not only did Christ come, but men had been prepared to appreciate Him when He came. Jesus did not bring in a different religion from that of Hosea and Isaiah, but He brought in the perfect stage of it; and it is for this reason that He Himself, in reading the Old Testament, heard God's voice as He read, and found that earlier revelation to be a means for Him of fellowship with the Father.

(2) There is the historical development of mankind. The unity and the character of God is enough by itself to justify Christians in finding revelation here. God is made known through the moral order on which specifically human life reposes, and most of all through conscience. He is found in the confirmation afforded by history to the maxim that "righteousness exalteth a nation." In a still loftier degree He is found in

the lives and teachings of great religious personalities; there, indeed, He is seen most clearly outside the Bible, as it is also through such heroic figures that some fragments of spiritual truth have been most widely propagated. And yet with regard to the spiritual effect of these non-Christian pioneers, two remarks, I think, must be added. In the first place, religious phenomena in the non-Christian world display no steady or consistent advance; isolated spots of light appear, but surrounded by impenetrable darkness. Secondly, such progress as other faiths exhibit is invariably the result of their transcending the founder, whereas in the case of Christianity revival and forward movement always flow from regained touch with Jesus.

On the other hand, heathenism (if that word be permissible) is negatively full of lessons. The fact that its nobler elements have so often sunk into baser things like nature-worship, idolatry, unrelieved formalism; the emergence of varied plausible but fruitless efforts at self-redemption, the alternatives to Jesus Christ being as it were successively tried in advance and found wanting—all this has gone to prepare the world for a religion in which men are called not to earn the forgiving love of God, but to receive it.

(3) There is the revelation of Nature. It is of course undeniable that people exist to whom Nature, from the religious point of view, presents an obscuring screen rather than a transparent

THE IDEA OF REVELATION

medium; and in this age devoted to intensified scientific study of the animate world, an age whose higher thought is typified by Tennyson, they have probably been more numerous than in any modern generation. None the less, we may venture on two assertions. First, to some and even to many persons God does appear in the splendour and loveliness of the physical world. They have a real experience of Him; they feel, as Wordsworth felt among the great mountains, the power of an unseen and eternal Presence. In hours of vision they discern behind and within the greatness and the glory of the material universe a diviner greatness and a diviner glory. Secondly, it is only in the light of Christ that Nature's message can be deciphered clearly. Apart from Him, we should scarcely know what to make of the world. Begin with Nature, remain her scholar exclusively, and she will take you but a little way; for the first question of personal religion, What must I do to be saved? is one to which Nature gives no distinct reply.

On the other hand, the man who has beheld and worshipped God in Christ can see more deeply into the life of things. Out of the aspect of the natural world, its starry heavens, its revolving seasons, he draws a profound and calming sense of the Divine faithfulness. "Heaven and earth," one has written, "are not only a picture of God's omnipotence; they tell us, with a sublime communicative confidence, that without hasting, without resting, He will do as He has said."

CHAPTER IV

THE BIBLICAL CONCEPTION OF GOD

WHAT we gather out of the Biblical literature is not so much an articulated theory of the Divine Being, as a believing presentation of the living God in the light of His redeeming action. There is a gradual manifesting of the judgment and mercy present in God for the sinful, and this manifestation is so disposed as to lead up to that which is also its interpretation and its seal—the person of Jesus Christ. Thus in the Bible the idea of God which believers hold, or rather which holds and masters them, has history as its fruitful background and medium. Nowhere is there even the suggestion of formal articles of belief having been inserted, by some preternatural mechanism, in the devout mind. Everything in man's relation to God, hence too everything in man's apprehension of God, is as it were lived out in the concrete happenings of time, before being consciously shaped in doctrine.

It therefore is vain to expect that the Bible will exhibit one unvarying and rigidly fixed conception of God on its first page and its last. What we *are* entitled to look for is that the trend of Biblical teaching shall be all in one direction; and he would be a bold man who contended that, if the facts be viewed largely, this is not what they indicate. Sheer uniformity is a different matter.

THE BIBLICAL CONCEPTION OF GOD

The Bible as a whole represents the living converse of God with men; and just as our impressions of a friend deepen and intensify as a result of his successive words and actions, so the Gospel of St John, with so much revealing history behind it, has truth to tell about God richer by far than can be found, say, in the Book of Judges. Indeed, the more faithfully the Biblical documents represent the different ages of which they profess to be the record, the plainer ought to be the marks upon them of the Divinely-guided advance from less to more worthy ideas of the Eternal. His dealings with men from century to century are not without gain. Time is necessary for the appropriation of the truth He utters to man; but time and His unresting grace being given, the ages do bring a heightening, enrichment, and universalization of earlier thought. The human mind has always been apt to insist that religious truth should all have entered the world together, *en bloc*, by a single impulse. Thus it has often been argued that all the Psalms must have been written by David, although this means condemning to silence whole generations of the ancient Jewish Church. That is not God's way. First the blade, then the ear, after that the full corn in the ear. We may say of the growing apprehension of God within the Bible, as Proverbs does of the path of the just, that it is " as the shining light, which shineth more and more unto the perfect day."

Now this fact that the idea of God has developed in time is occasionally given, at the hands of

THE CHRISTIAN APPREHENSION OF GOD

unsympathetic critics, an extremely prejudicial turn. As happens constantly in related fields, the history of an idea is employed to discredit its validity. The argument, put shortly, is to the effect that if religious thought in Israel passed through various stages, some more primitive, some less—if, for example, at one time Jahveh was regarded as ruling over Israel while simultaneously Chemosh ruled over Moab, so that the grand truth of ethical and universal monotheism dawned slowly and only by degrees filled the sky—how then, it is asked with great emphasis, can we attach the least importance to a conception with such a pedigree ? Is it not rendered invalid simply by its own past ? Must it not to the end retain something of the inadequacy of its early stages ?

But it is mere delusion to suppose that the idea of God is at all singular in having had a chequered past. Science is here in the same condemnation as faith, if condemnation it be. Present-day science is the lineal descendant of that current a thousand years ago, and the science of the Middle Ages was crude enough in all conscience ; but no intelligent person now thinks the worse of astronomy because it grew from astrology, or of chemistry because alchemy was its raw and credulous predecessor. Things are what they are and not what they come from. Every idea of real importance for the modern mind started from humble origins. Number, justice, marriage, music, love, the State—not an idea, pursuit, or institution can be named of which man's primeval notions

THE BIBLICAL CONCEPTION OF GOD

were not, from the standpoint of later times, utterly rudimentary. But no one supposes that because there are Australian aborigines who cannot count beyond five (some travellers say four), therefore later developments of mathematics are of no value, and Einstein a self-deceived visionary. We do not argue that a concert of tom-toms in Central Africa is the best of which music is capable, or that a symphony of Beethoven is somehow covered with disrepute because amongst its ancestors must be reckoned that comparatively tuneless and barbaric noise. Why then should the idea of God be the worse for its history? What we have to fix clearly in our minds is the principle that nothing scholars may elicit as to the stages or influences through which the consciousness of God was quickened by the Divine Spirit in Old Testament believers in the least affects the truth or value of the conception of God, now that it is here. It was certain beforehand that the Absolute Reality would at first be indicated or named in words even more imperfect than those we ourselves use; for these grey fathers of the world, like us, were throwing out their minds in response to an infinite object, not surveying or measuring it exactly.

In its first sentence, the Old Testament takes the being and the transcendence of God for granted. His reality or unity is never considered by the great prophets as a subject needing to be discussed; and, as it has been put, "there is but

One God, not because it happens to be so, but because it cannot be otherwise." We do not institute careful inquiries as to the real existence of our friends—not a perfect analogy, as anyone can see, but at all events fit to remind us that the prophets start from the assumption that God has spoken, with a grace that is imperious as well as loving, has laid His hand upon them, and is sending them forth on His errands. Atheism is, speaking broadly, a modern product; and it seems always to be a result of concentrating attention on the evil of the world and passing over the good as if it called for no explanation, but somehow produced itself.

At various points in the earlier books of the Old Testament it is possible to detect vestiges and even survivals of the natural soil on which a genuinely spiritual view of God was being superinduced. The notion that Canaan is literally God's dwelling-place; that His anger can be appeased by the smoke of sacrifice; that the massacre of a whole tribe could be His will—these things are relics of the pagan natural religion against which the great prophets fought sternly. The more steadily indeed we contemplate these curious residual elements, the more vividly do we realize that nothing but the self-revealing action of God could have lifted human faith to a higher plane. Belief in a God who enjoins massacre could never *of itself* flower into belief in the Lord who, like a father, is pitiful to his children.[1]

[1] Ps. ciii. 13.

THE BIBLICAL CONCEPTION OF GOD

Whatever the difficulty of choosing our words, we are compelled to say that more is here than " natural evolution." Revelation is creative. In Israel, as a matter of fact, the higher faith had to struggle for its life against the ingrained paganism of the masses which, so far from giving birth to true monotheism, would have strangled it in its cradle. Everything in Israel's environment went to foster polytheism; the newness of the prophetic message had its source in the Divine initiative.

Twenty years since many scholars were unwilling to regard the authentic Hebrew faith as older than Moses; but, though undoubtedly the prophets love to dwell on the Exodus as opening the great epoch, the most untrammelled inquirers have at the moment a somewhat deeper respect for the story of Abraham and his heroic obedience to God's call. Still, for a bird's-eye view of the whole, which is all we are attempting now, such details are of no account. The Exodus marks the revolutionizing interposition by which Jahveh constituted Israel His people. Prophets divined the nature of God largely through what He had accomplished for the nation. Throughout the centuries one cardinal relationship holds between the parties to the covenant—Jahveh the God of Israel, Israel the people of Jahveh. It was a covenant, let us not forget, made and maintained by God. All writers moreover are agreed in teaching that from the outset elements of a genuinely ethical sort belonged to the conception of Jahveh. " There was at least on His nature a crescent of light, which waxed until it overspread His face, and He was light with no darkness at all." The jealousy, for example, so frequently ascribed to Him is an imaginative—and surely even yet a quite intelligible—symbol of that intolerance which higher moral ideas must always manifest to those that are lower. Nothing has been of higher value for the progress of mankind than, on the one hand, sexual purity, on the other, social justice; and it is significant that Jahveh is so early represented as inexorably antagonistic to infractions of these laws. Very early too the principle is announced that obedience is in His sight better than sacrifice.

The task of the writing prophets, from Amos onwards, was not merely to preach a new faith; it might with equal truth be said to be that of compelling their hearers to face the implications of the theocentric faith by which the best minds had long been inspired. Perpetually they spoke of God and His claim upon men; they pointed ever to the character of the sublime Power who was more and more unveiling Himself in the vicissitudes of Israel's history, as the spiritual education of chosen souls within the nation proceeded. He was One who interwove Himself with their experience, and was indeed "the living and true God." Thus, as teaching came line upon line, and precept upon precept, the conviction forced itself home on moral grounds that Jahveh is the God of the whole earth. Israel indeed was His covenant-people, but only in view of a great purpose, viz.,

THE BIBLICAL CONCEPTION OF GOD

that they might publish His name to the Gentiles. Those who have raised the question whether it is credible that Jesus' missionary horizon ever extended beyond the Jews might profitably have reflected that long before the world-mission of Israel had become clear to the vision of Old Testament saints and seers.

One or two illustrations may now be given of what, roughly but not altogether inaccurately, we may call the individual contributions of different prophets to the full Old Testament conception of God. Thus Amos burnt it into Israel's heart that God is absolute righteousness, that He is (so to express it) the moral law alive; and to this all-determining truth he added the proclamation that the service or oblation which Jahveh requires of His people is a corresponding rectitude of life. Hosea, on the other hand, is the preacher of the Divine love, changeless and unwearied, a love not to be repelled or quenched by any unworthiness or infidelity of its object; for him "Jehovah's love to His own is the deepest thing in religion, and every problem of faith centres in it." Isaiah returns over and over to the majesty of God; in his superb poetry he is ever dwelling on Jahveh as the transcendent and world-controlling Monarch, absolute and without a rival in His right to the allegiance of men. Jeremiah, most Christian of all the prophets, unless we bracket Hosea along with him, shows ethical monotheism at the full; and it is in keeping with this perfected monotheism that he more than any should bring out with a haunting tenderness the personal relation of God to the single soul. Ezekiel, who has been described as a priest in a prophet's mantle, in some degree throws back to earlier conceptions; like Isaiah, he is absorbed by Jahveh's supramundane glory, and insists on the immediate moral responsibility that in consequence attaches to each man in His sight.

These of course are only the broadest of characterizations; but they serve a purpose if they help us to realize that the history of Israel, in its deepest vein, was marked by a growing apprehension of God, alike in His goodness and His severity. And with regard to them all, two facts, as has been pointed out, have to be borne in mind: first, that a prophet is not to be held as ignoring one side of God's nature because he speaks chiefly of some other; and secondly, that " the prophetic ideas form but one-half of the prophetic teaching, the greater half lies in their own life and their personal relation to God." And yet even in reading these great spokesmen for God, on whose truth the world is living to this hour, we cannot altogether forget that a Greater was still to come; One who was a prophet and more. In a striking passage Dr Cairns insists on the unlikeness between the prophets in their relationship to the truth they brought and Jesus Christ as inseparable from *His* disclosure of God. " When we think of Amos, we think of his stern message of God's Justice, and with Hosea we associate the message of God's Love. But the converse is

THE BIBLICAL CONCEPTION OF GOD

untrue. When we think of the Righteousness of God or of His Love, who remembers either Hosea or Amos ? But when we think of God as 'the Father,' we think at once of 'the Son'."[1]

Already in the prophets we become aware of the awe-inspiring and fundamental paradox that runs through all Biblical thought concerning God. We may regard this paradox from either end. The God of awful majesty is the God of tender mercy—that is one aspect; the God of tender mercy is also the God of awful majesty—that is the other. Nor must we separate these two sides; each aspect needs the other and ultimately rests upon it. The majesty of God sheds its burning glow on every page the prophets write, but it may be surmised even more impressively from the personal attitude they as religious men take to Him. They are humbled to the dust in His presence. They speak of Him with a reverence scarcely to be uttered by human tongue. He comes in storm and flame to break in pieces all the powers of earth; once His purpose has been fixed, no resistance can avail, but all must fall before His feet. All peoples, all ages, are swept into His triumphant plan. There are fear-inspiring elements in this God; His will is inviolable and His commandments break and grind to powder every hostile force. Yet against this, like a silver lining to a dark cloud, stand those qualities to which the devout heart can fasten its confidence. Under His wings the children of men find refuge; He is

[1] *Christianity in the Modern World*, p. 44.

a strong rock to those who trust in His great name. He will bring His cause to victory by making His dwelling-place with men; for the infinite Lord of Hosts is also the compassionate God of Jacob. The two aspects of God are in the strictest sense correlative; remove either, and all meaning fades from the other. "Thus saith the high and lofty One that inhabiteth eternity, whose name is Holy; I dwell in the high and holy place, with him also that is of a contrite and humble spirit, to revive the spirit of the humble, and to revive the heart of the contrite ones."[1] Only he knows the mercy of God who has trembled at His glorious power.

As we review the long story and mark the broadening and deepening flow of believing insight, we can better understand what is really meant for religion by a truer, loftier, and more worthy conception of God. It distinctly does not mean a conception fit for use in exact scientific theology. In scientific theology the prophets show no interest. Ancient Semitic thought, at least in its best representatives, has a passion for unity; science, which deals inductively with the multiplicity of phenomena, lay outside its range. Hence the prophets, those classical exponents of faith, were never disposed to measure the elevation or completeness of their thought of God by its capacity to figure in a purely scientific argument. Or again, it has occasionally been imagined that you reach a higher idea of God in

[1] Isa. lvii. 15.

THE BIBLICAL CONCEPTION OF GOD

proportion as you have purged it of all elements which with any show of reason can be called anthropomorphic—modelled, that is to say, directly on human experience. All phrases must be eliminated, for example, that allude to God's arm, or His ear, or His heart; care must be taken lest He should be conceived of in terms of human feeling and purpose. But neither does this suit the prophets. They indulge in anthropomorphisms of the most startling kind; indeed, they ascribe to Jahveh every emotion except fear and a sense of bodily danger. Hosea can represent God as saying of His dealings with men: "I taught Ephraim to go, I took them on my arms"[1]— words of which metaphysic can make nothing. But for religion they are of vital importance, implying as they do that God is not far away from men but near; He is actually among them, entering into their childish needs and taking their burdens on Himself. What the conception of God may become when once the life-blood of anthropomorphism has been drained out, we see in the God of Mohammed. The Deity pictured in the Koran is " like the desert, monotonous and barren, an unfigured surface, an unresponsive immensity." Even what may be called His favour toward Mohammedans, real as it is felt to be, is in itself quite inscrutable and passionless. At this point we recognize how Islam has fallen, in its religious range of thought, far below the level of Old Testament prophecy, let alone the teaching

[1] Hos. xi. 3 (R.V).

THE CHRISTIAN APPREHENSION OF GOD

of Christ. Just through picture and emblem, not in spite of them, Biblical writers opened vistas into the being of God which so far have been only partially explored.

The question whether the Fatherhood of God is taught in the Old Testament is scarcely more than a matter of words. The best minds certainly had caught a flying glimpse of it, at the least; yet here exaggeration must be avoided, otherwise we shall find it hard to explain to ingenuous minds what difference in this regard, if any, was made by Jesus. Increasing stress was all along being laid on God's relation to individuals; but this had never been wholly ignored, and quite indefensible things have often been said by scholars about the mere submergence of the single life in group or tribe at more primitive levels of worship. If the individual at first counted for next to nothing, it becomes a mystery how the great pioneering figures of Old Testament faith could ever raise their heads or gather disciples. But admitting all that, I can scarcely go whole-heartedly with the writer who declares that "what human language can express concerning the love of God for man we find already uttered in the Old Testament." In one sense, doubtless, this is true; in another sense, it ignores what is the most important fact of all. Thus the 23rd Psalm speaks of God's fatherly care for men in language of the most profound and moving character. The tender words men learn as children, and they repeat them secretly in age. Yet nothing is more certain

THE BIBLICAL CONCEPTION OF GOD

than that the beautiful relationship depicted in the Psalm is felt to be confined to members of the Chosen People. The writer would have denied that his words held true of a Greek or a Persian; such persons were outside the covenant, and God's attitude towards them was at best a matter of grave uncertainty. It is due solely to Jesus that into this Psalm of psalms we can read such infinite meanings that it becomes a sacred vehicle of our hope in God.

The period between the Old Testament and the New is not to be considered, as has been done by too many, a wilderness of bigotry, in which the religious mind wandered long and found no way. It was at least an age when the individual more and more came to his own in religion, and as a consequence real progress was made in eschatological insight. No such greater gains can be pointed to in the thought of God by which leading minds were dominated. The idea, rather, is in danger of becoming petrified, of losing the wonderful *naïveté*, ardour, and urgency of prophetic religion. Jahveh is conceived as infinitely sublime, but also as infinitely distant. His throne is above the heavens, and not seldom we learn that His tabernacle no longer is among men. His way now is to send messengers upon earth rather than His own living Spirit, to touch and change men's hearts. Especially in Hellenistic Judaism the anthropomorphisms of the Old Testament are studiously explained away in terms of allegory, and their place taken by a somewhat abstract conception shorn of much that had given to the vision of Jahveh its concrete and vital aspect. As a result it is felt that living revelation has been suspended, and men look for the declaration of God's will more to canonical books than to His personal message spoken by inspired men. We have therefore to reckon with the fact that in the Judaism contemporary with our Lord there prevailed a view of the Divine nature characterized by excessive blankness and (as it were) thinness of internal life, remotely supreme, and severed from the world by a wide gulf. Curiously enough, this was combined with a fondness for quaint and even grotesque theological fancies, as when God Himself is represented as being engaged day and night in the study of the Law, and not of the Law merely, but of the rabbinic commentaries.

When, however, we set up this background as the foil against which can best be seen the greatness of the revelation mediated by Jesus, let us recollect that this is not the whole story. Lindsay has said that when Luther came forward at the Reformation, what he did was to bring out, and take as the staple of his message, the old evangelical beliefs which had never died out of the medieval Church, however they may have been banished from the mechanized technical statement of the dogmas on which the intellect could sharpen itself, but which were out of all relation to the practical religious life of men. In the same way, although in our Lord's lifetime there was much in the prevailing doctrinal temper which He was

THE BIBLICAL CONCEPTION OF GOD

compelled to censure, with strong and scathing words, there was also a vein of simple and devout piety to which His message made a direct appeal. He felt no need to proclaim a new conception, in the broad sense, but could say, as reported in the Fourth Gospel, " Ye believe in God, believe also in me."[1] None the less, the outcome of His being in the world was that, when men looked up into the Divine Face, they saw there a new and previously undiscerned expression.

It must always strike us as in the highest degree unlikely that there should have been no original and distinctive feature in Jesus' greatest gift to the world, viz., His presentation of God. One on whom the wonder of redemption has laid its spell is naturally disconcerted when told that the main new thought by which he lives—the thought of God—was in no sense modified, enriched, or perfected by Him who made the Christian life possible. Jesus taught no new God, as Mohammed did in a later age ; but this is entirely congruous with the certainty that He opened a new and final stage in the apprehension of faith's great object. The dull, intrinsically uninspiring suggestion that the high-water mark in human conceptions of the Divine had been reached before Jesus, that His view of God was completely familiar, and that His part lay merely in confirming truth already known and registered, may therefore be put side.

At this point it may be said : Yes, in Jesus'

[1] John xiv. 1.

thought of God there *is* a new element, and it is the doctrine of the Trinity. He was the first to teach that God is triune Spirit. Let it be observed that the question here is not whether the doctrine of the Trinity is a true doctrine. For my own part, I believe that a genuinely Trinitarian view of God can hardly be evaded by those who try to think out and think through the ultimate problems of Christian faith, and that he who would express all that the believing mind envisages in God must say: Father, Son, and Holy Spirit. But, I repeat, that is not our question now. The question, strictly, is whether the doctrine of the Trinity is a primary utterance with Jesus, and not rather an implication of the experience into which He leads. It really is impossible to read the Gospels freshly and gain the impression that when Jesus spoke of God, or presented God through action, the thought in the foreground of His mind, that which He chiefly longed for men to grasp and make their own, was the thought of God in three persons.

In what direction then shall we turn? To answer this question, let us recall the fact that Jesus' new revelation of God, in whatever it consisted, was not conveyed solely or even mainly by words. It is a saying of Goethe: " The Highest cannot be spoken." This is undeniable, but for ourselves we may add, "None the less it may be lived out in act, in personal being." As may be gathered from His institution of the Lord's Supper, a point came where, in the endeavour to show men how the Cross meant sacrifice, and how only through unity with His indwelling life that sacrifice could bless them, Jesus passed clean beyond words; in the poet's phrase, His meaning " broke through language and escaped." So too, even if His revelation of God used no new *words* for its expression, over and above all that there still remains the greater revelation enshrined in life and act. Every good man is greater far than anything he may say, and this is true supremely of Christ. Whatever be thought of the novelty of His terms, at least in Him a new Word, a new utterance of God's nature took flesh and dwelt among us. " It was not so much what He said," Harnack writes, " but how He said it, and how in Him it became spirit and life." A new realization of God appeared on earth with elemental power. Behind every word of Jesus stands the wonder of Himself. His disclosure of God is original, familiar though the language may often be, just as *In Memoriam* is a new creation, despite the fact that every word in the poem had existed before in the dictionary. In Him the redeeming God grew apprehensible through the unforgettable realities—intimate yet mysterious, mysterious yet intimate—of human character.

But more. Jesus' revelation of God stands by itself in virtue of a new purity and inner consistence. Grant the possibility that a verbal parallel for everything He said might be produced from Jewish sages, yet He left out lower things formerly put in and thus presented the essential nucleus of the truth in such a form as to make their reassertion, if it should ever be attempted, a manifest incongruity. It is indisputable that Pharisaism had declared a noble thought of God's goodness and holiness. But unhappily it had added much that justly created doubt. What is it to me that men call God holy if on the next page they picture Him as unholy, as valuing sacrifice more than mercy, outward forms more than inward love? The untrue element overclouds the true, infecting it with its own untrustworthiness and robbing the whole of convincing power. Under these conditions, to give a pure thought of God—to exhibit God to the moral consciousness as light with no darkness at all—is in a vital sense to give a new thought. But such a pure, unified presentation can come only through a pure, unified life. Thus we return to our commanding principle that words, merely as words, will not suffice. The vision of God apprehended nineteen centuries ago, which the Christian mind is still striving to explore, rose out of all that Jesus was known to have been.

We may find the new conception expressed most clearly, so far as words avail, in a name which the Gospel of St John reports from Jesus' lips, as used by Him in prayer. It is "Holy Father."[1] Holiness, long known as a Divine attribute, now takes on a new colour from association with perfect Fatherhood. But the combination is something

[1] John xvii. 11; in verse 25 the words are "righteous Father."

THE BIBLICAL CONCEPTION OF GOD

which in height and depth, in length and breadth, had never before been realized. How is this?

The term " Father " is found in the Old Testament, which even speaks of God in a significant phrase as " the Father of the fatherless." But the meaning of a name is measured by what we have learned to put into it, since there is no word in all human speech that explains itself. I have known of a man who protested he never could bear to hear God called " Father "—the name awoke such dreadful memories. What dawns gradually on us as we read the Gospels is that God is such a Father as evokes from Jesus a constant, reverential loving trust; He is *a Father worthy even of the perfect trust of Jesus.* Or, to approach the matter from a slightly different angle, the Fatherhood of God is reflected in, and corresponds to, the Sonship of Jesus. So we, like the angels in 1st Peter,[1] may bend down and peer into the mirror of our Lord's life and passion; and there it is the Father that we see.

It is sober truth to say that if we are to reach a distinct and redeeming impression of the Fatherhood of God, it is through Christ alone it can be attained. " No man cometh unto the Father but by me," is a faithful transcript of the fact. It is not bravado or petulance or error; it is how things happen. Obviously enough it was not left to Jesus to manifest God in the character of Creator, or of supreme Moral Authority, or of Sustainer of the world. Long before His time,

[1] 1 Pet. i. 12.

THE CHRISTIAN APPREHENSION OF GOD

these ideas had become the possession of many. It *was* left to Jesus to manifest God in the character of holy and loving Fatherhood. We are debtors to Him for the revolutionizing knowledge that the Holy One is love to all men whatsoever, nor, apart from Him, would this be credible even yet to multitudes who deeply realize the world's immeasurable pain or know the agonies of the conscience-stricken. None are so well aware of this as missionaries. In the words of one who has given his life to China : " Take away Jesus, and there may remain a graven image (popular religion), or an Unknowable First Cause (philosophical religion), but not a Heavenly Father."[1] Jesus put this faith in men's hearts, and only contact with Him keeps it alive to-day. Once given, the revelation that had made all things new of necessity threw back its own colour on the ideas of Creatorship and Sovereignty, imparting to them the warmth and nearness of Love.

In the closing verses of the Book of Jonah a long step is undoubtedly taken towards the unveiling of the Divine Fatherhood. The words, spoken to a Jew by the God of Israel : " Should not I have pity on Nineveh ? " may be read as extending the Fatherly care of God over all men, without exception. It is the note which Jesus prolongs and deepens. The lost prodigal, who is kissed and feasted and given back his self-respect, is not merely a lost Jew ; he is the lost man, the wandering child wherever found, and however late

[1] O'Neill, *The Quest for God in China*, p. 260.

his penitent return to the old home. It has been justly remarked that there is no passage in the Gospels where our Lord directly speaks of God as the Father of. all; yet we need be under no real uncertainty on the point whether His attitude to all is fatherly. This is proved to the hilt by the fact that Christ, just because He was conscious being God's Representative, " received sinners " ; and received them simply on the ground of their need of God. We best understand the universal character of the Divine Fatherhood by observing Jesus' treatment of the individual; for here the individual is the universal—he is man *as man*. Our Lord lived in a day when the Divine holiness was commonly pictured as purely menacing and paralysing to the unworthy, and none but the good (it was thought) might approach the Most High. How did Jesus meet this and disown it ? Not by denying the purity of holiness but by His loving welcome of the guilty. We watch His eager forgiveness of the paralytic, His open friendship with Zaccheus, His infinitely sensitive and understanding attitude to the woman that was a sinner, His wonderful love to the dying thief ; and as we look on we say : Thus God will receive me, if I ask to be received. God shines to us through it all—a God of grace who will make no terms with evil, yet takes the guilty to His heart.

God is so much a Father that He receives sinners. It looks as if nothing more remained to be said, and yet I think there is something more. To receive is one thing ; to go out in search of

THE CHRISTIAN APPREHENSION OF GOD

the lost is another. And the greatest thing we learn from Christ is that in Him the Father is seeking out His erring and dying children. He searches for them at His own cost and reckons no sacrifice too vast to pay for their recovery. In other words, we fail to apprehend the whole meaning enshrined by Jesus in the name " Holy Father " until our minds open to the vast practical consequences which this presentation of the Father had for Jesus' own life and which, from an indefinitely early point in His career, He perceived that it must have. Throughout we have been guided by the principle that revelation comes supremely through living experience. But the climax of Jesus' experience was the Cross. And if it be true that at every step He let loose another secret of God's love ; if in every act, every event, every burden from His cradle to His grave we find the Father's love stealing out somewhere, then Calvary is the cardinal element in Jesus' exposition of the Fatherhood of God. For He went to death in perfect unity and agreement with the Father's mind. In other words, by dying thus in behalf of men He unveiled a Fatherhood of such dimensions —so broad and deep and high—that at the last Divine sacrifice comes into it. Old Testament religion had been rich in pictures of the Divine compassion ; but even there the thought had never arisen of a love willing to surrender itself to death for men. It had spoken of redemption, but it had not disclosed how much redemption was to cost ; and by disclosing it our Lord drew

THE BIBLICAL CONCEPTION OF GOD

back the curtain, and gave one glimpse of the Father's heart which solves all difficulty and removes all fear. We need not at the moment discuss theories of the atonement; but, on any terms which represent a real continuity with the faith of the New Testament, we cannot say less than that the love present in Christ's death for sin is the love of God. There the pure passion flows forth which has throbbed in God's heart from all eternity; and the holiness there manifested, which awes the heart by its final reaction against evil, is the very holiness of God Himself. "Holiness" and "love," as we now use these terms to define the nature of the Eternal, are interpreted for us above all by Jesus' great act in bearing man's sin. Thus Christ's experience in its fullness shows how we must think of God.

When the apostles use the distinctively Christian name, " the God and Father of our Lord Jesus Christ," they are doing what human language can do to express all this; but also they are doing something more. We cannot forget that to them Jesus, though He had died, was no longer dead. He was the Risen One; and no one can read the Epistles without making the discovery that for the apostolic mind the Resurrection had changed everything. For what did the Resurrection mean? It meant, to begin with, that God the Father had responded to the perfect trust of the Son. That victory over the grave was no mere strange portent; it was on God's part a moral act, on

THE CHRISTIAN APPREHENSION OF GOD

Christ's a moral experience, by which utter faith was vindicated. Jesus the Believer was acknowledged by the Father, the seal of Divine acceptance being set upon His sacrifice and death for men. In the second place, it was the vindication of the Father no less than of the Son. Once and for all it was shown that God is as omnipotent as He is loving. His grace and His power are alike mighty to save. Had Jesus' experience ended with the grave, Christianity would have been very different from the religion we know, if indeed it would ever have existed. We should scarcely describe it, as faith ever since has done, as the religion of joy. For it would have rested on a different thought of God. He would then have failed to meet the final challenge of death.

The Biblical conception of God, thus completed and crowned, was afterwards half-lost for centuries; but not at least while the men survived who had known Christ. Right through the documents of the New Testament we can trace the sweeping change it wrought. To St Paul and St John, always, God is holy and almighty Father. Something—describe it as we may—has happened to persuade them of this in an irreversible manner; something that compelled them once and for all to have done with every other interpretation. Always, too, that something is the Cross and Resurrection. At the vital centre of religion, they are unflinchingly true to Jesus' mind. They believe in a God who has been decisively revealed in His Son and unceasingly communicates His life

THE BIBLICAL CONCEPTION OF GOD

to men by His Spirit. This idea for them is no necessary truth of reason, won by dint of hard thinking, nor is it a commonplace of natural piety; it simply is a revelation. It is a truth which has broken on the human mind through a particular person who had a particular career, and to the end it will depend for its vital force on Him who first mediated it to the world. "God was in Christ reconciling the world unto Himself" —so long as this great confession is uttered by thankful hearts, the new thought of God will live and celebrate its triumphs over doubt and fear.

But the new thought is still a living thought, not one which can be printed in a book and handed on as a dead piece of information. Of it supremely Goethe's word holds true, that we inherit it only as we win it for ourselves. To believe it is for each man the venture of life. None can have Christ's thought of God who will not in faith dare to have it. It is only in His company, face to face with One who knew Himself to be the Son, that any of us can learn freshly how a disciple must think of the Father. "Speak not of God's goodness if it has not cast you at the feet of Christ."

CHAPTER V

THE PERSONALITY OF GOD

At no point in our argument is it more essential than here to recollect that Theology is not so much a creative as an interpretative study. Its business is to make explicit the truth which faith contains implicitly, not to introduce the Christian mind to truth about God hitherto unfamiliar. Our one aim must be to lead faith to a clearer consciousness of its own nature and meaning. With respect to our present topic, the personality of God, what is required is much less to offer an independent proof that God is personal in nature than, first, to exhibit the conception of Divine personality as filling a decisive place in Christian belief, and, in the second place, to repel objections to this position which serious thinkers have put forward.

Our first question must therefore be whether in the Christian view God *is* personal. What is the living heart of Christian belief ? It is the consciousness of being redeemed into fellowship with God through Jesus Christ. Now, it is fairly clear, this experience is possible only if there can be personal communion between God and us, between the " Thou " of heaven and the " I " of earth. It is personal communion, because it can be nothing lower or less without ceasing to be itself, and because no idea can be formed of anything higher. The religious interests of the

THE PERSONALITY OF GOD

case have justice done to them only if we lay down that there does exist such a thing as definite and spiritual intercourse between God and man; though we must of course add that in this relationship, alike for inception and continuance, the absolute initiative and supremacy is with God. The holy love which comes home to us in Christ, as a Divine attitude or influence bearing on us directly, not in the mass merely but individually, is something to which no significance can be attached unless it is the expression of a Power, spiritual in being, which acts with self-consciousness and self-determination; and for such a Power we have no name but personality. If we are forbidden to employ the idea of "personal being" to represent the Power revealed in the love of Christ to the sinful, every real possibility of representing that Power in thought is taken away.

Love, with its movement between person and person, is of course not the only experience which points in this direction. The same may be said of human faith, penitence, prayer, the sense of religious obligation. All these are meaningless save on certain terms. It is indeed no exaggeration to say that with the vanishing of belief in the personality of God there must vanish the whole round of spiritual life of which faith, love, and prayer are vital functions, except in some verbal sense which would be obviously far-fetched and unnatural. Faith, as self-renouncing trust in the Highest, is an attitude I can take solely to a Being

THE CHRISTIAN APPREHENSION OF GOD

of whom I can predicate a living interest in my lot; obligation, conceived religiously, cannot in its loftiest form be or be defined apart from relations of a " personal " kind; and prayer, to be more than soliloquy, involves (at least in its Christian intention) that God hears and knows what I say. For our present purpose, too great emphasis cannot be laid on prayer. All Christians who pray fervently have a quite overwhelming sense of the Divine personality. You may speculate on the Divine, or dream of the Divine, or aspire to the Divine, or swoon into the Divine without raising our issue, or even after reaching a negative conclusion upon it; but one thing you cannot do—you cannot pray in Christ's name, or after His example, unless the Divine be a living personal Spirit. Henry Ward Beecher somewhere writes: "When the down-shining of the Holy Ghost comes to me, I know by an evidence within myself that is unspeakably more convincing to me than eye or hand or ear can be, that there is a God and that He is my God." " He is my God "—there is the basal certitude. We may fix it then, without further argument, that the personality of God is a vital concern of Christian faith, in any form of it which remains true to type. It accredits itself as a quality of Ultimate Being without which Christian religion could have neither truth nor value. Accordingly, when faith begins to take stock of its own contents, it at once singles out this characteristic of God, that He is personal, by a luminous and unhesitating intuition.

THE PERSONALITY OF GOD

In these circumstances, it might have been expected that even thinkers who reject the personality of God, as speculatively incredible, would have readily conceded that, as a conviction, it is bound up inextricably with the religion of the Bible. Doubtless in most cases they have done so. But not always. Matthew Arnold had much of an exceptionally stimulating kind to say about the Bible; but it was perhaps one of his least felicitous suggestions that in the Bible God is not a personal Spirit, but " a stream of tendency, not ourselves, making for righteousness." Such an idea really could have been put forward only by a thinker to whom the conception of revelation had become unmeaning; and it is akin, so far, to the crying fault of that great book, *Ecce Homo*, namely, the absence of a chapter, or even a substantial paragraph, concerning Jesus' thought of God. But we need no more try to draw a circle without a centre than describe the religion of Jesus Christ without reference to God. No serious student of Scripture could regard Arnold's or Seeley's view as anything but the result of unhappy prejudice. Whether God is personal or not, that at least is how the Biblical writers thought of Him; while not of course employing our modern category of " personality," they assumed that God is such that with Him man can have personal relationships, and that true religion can exist on this basis and no other. What *is* the Bible but the personal converse of God and man, and how could this be so unless the nature of the inter-

THE CHRISTIAN APPREHENSION OF GOD

locutors was, in some decisive way, identical in quality? As has been said truly: "The Bible is charged with the supreme truths which speak to every believing heart, the clear voice of God's love so tender and personal and simple that a child can understand it." Accordingly, that particular thinkers should have rejected belief in the Divine personality on their own account is intelligible enough, even if we may deem their reasons bad; but how they should have supposed that in rejecting it they had the Bible on their side all but passes comprehension, and it is probably this flagrant error on Arnold's part that helped to deprive him of much of the influence which, in theology, he unquestionably merited.

All believers of the Biblical type, all inspired by the distinctive kind of religion which the Hebrew prophets inculcate, have so lived in fellowship with God that to raise the question of His personal being would have appeared to them superfluous. We do not raise that issue about a friend; and the Scripture verse which calls Abraham "the Friend of God"[1] points to an infinitely sublimer power of friendship on God's part. Only when speculative difficulties have arisen does the problem become acute. Once it has forced itself to the front and become articulate, there can be of course no thought of stifling it; for violence in theology is the offspring of fear. In point of fact, it is to modern Pantheism that the distinction

[1] Jas. ii. 23.

THE PERSONALITY OF GOD

belongs of having met the idea of Divine personality with a fully reasoned denial. It is however remarkable—and this we may take as a point introductory to our survey of the negative argument—that no consistent thinker has ever found it possible to depersonalize God without having to depersonalize man as well; and personality is the one thing in our make-up which we are not willing to change or replace. The ideas of God and man vary together. Depreciation of the one is inevitably followed by a fall in value of the other. Hence, when Pantheism repudiated this basal tenet of Christianity on alleged philosophical grounds, it was to find that morality, whose interests it had been thought were not affected, instantly took up the challenge. At once it was felt that if you only persuade men that the Power supreme over the phenomenal universe is blind, deaf, and unresponsive, you cannot at will stop the argument just there. You are on an inclined plane and, whether or not you like it, you will slip lower down. Unavoidably you will be obliged to alter your view of man also; you will have no option but to conclude that even " the brave, the noble, and the wise " of our race are merely bits of Nature, easily replaceable parts of a vast unintelligent and aimless machine. Once the pantheistic argument has done its work, conscience no less than faith is obliged to breathe an atmosphere of poison. "When I see a young mother bending over her child," said a recent protagonist of Indian Pantheism, " I bow down before the image of God our mother. . . . When I see a harlot leaning down from her balcony, I bow before her also. I say, 'Behold the mother at her sport among the children of men.'" This is wholly logical for one to whom men are Gods and the imputation of sin a blasphemy.[1] Thus, in fighting its battle for the Divine personality, Christian faith has been defending the cause of morals equally with its own.

Let us now turn to one or two historically important instances of a philosophy in which the negative view has found clear expression. Personality, whatever else it involves, may best be recognized by the qualities of self-consciousness and self-determination. By the nature of the case, these two are inseparable. "Intelligence and Will are so intertwined that to attribute one to God cannot be done without also attributing the other." Now, it is precisely intelligence and will, in any reasonable and non-Pickwickian sense of these terms, that some of the most imposing speculative systems of the modern era have refused to ascribe to God. Spinoza is no materialist; yet he defines God as a Being consisting in neither mind nor matter, but manifested essentially in both these "attributes," and (this is the point) not more in one than in the other. Infinite thought, infinite extension—this is God, a vast and slumbering whole, without true freedom, or will, or love to man. This however must fail

[1] See Bicknell, *The Christian Idea of Sin and Original Sin*, pp. 91-2.

to satisfy the needs of conscience, not merely because nothing can be "bad" for such an all-embracing Substance, but because to Spinoza there is no more of God than there is of the world. Transcendence is here a meaningless term; infinite and finite are co-terminous; but in moral obligation we feel we are being *addressed from above*. As it has been put conclusively: "When I hear the voice of conscience within me, and I ask myself who spoke, if no better answer can be returned than I myself, I am still dissatisfied."[1] To Hegel, again, God is the Absolute Idea, pure thought in dynamical process of self-unfolding, the great dialectic alive. No one has ever been quite sure what Hegel believed about God. Some of his followers claimed him as a theist, indeed the first theist who had discovered how to do philosophical justice to Christianity. Others, like Strauss and Feuerbach, scouted the notion that his thought had the faintest resemblance to theism, and developed his argument by descending stages into a philosophy which has everything in common with materialism but the name. This at least means that Hegel's attitude to the idea of Divine personality was ambiguous in the extreme, and on such a point ambiguity suits Christian religion hardly better than sheer negation. Once more, to Schelling, at all events in his latest phase, the ground and principle of all is a blind, unforeseeing Somewhat, devoid of consciousness or will; a dim, mysterious chaos out of which

[1] J. B. Dalgairns, *Contemp. Rev.*, vol. xxiv., p. 328.

"God" struggles up by inches, disentangling Himself gradually—like Milton's "tawny lion, pawing to get free his hinder parts"—and *becoming* God as in due course He rises into independent being. "He sleeps in the plant," it has been said, "dreams in the animal, and only awakes to full intellectual and moral consciousness in the man. He would never in all probability have been conscious of His own being or of the world which He had produced but for the existence of man. In man He remembers what He fashioned in His sleep and in His dreams."[1]

We may reasonably conclude that each of these famous systems, varied as they may be, runs counter to the Christian thought of God as the Father of our Lord Jesus Christ, and our Father through Him. Or perhaps it would be truer to say that each contains factors which can be adjusted to the Christian idea of God only with intense difficulty. Spinoza, almost in so many words, removes all distinction between God and the world; Hegel (on the fairest interpretation) expounds a Deity that gains self-consciousness only in finite minds like our own; Schelling puts forward a conception which we not merely cannot think but which we see perfectly well to be unthinkable, viz., a Godhead that emerges out of growth, that is now but once was not, and, for all that such reasoning can prove, may again cease to be. Christian faith will never go shares with speculation of this kind, and the effort to

[1] Forbes Robinson, *The Self-Limitation of God*, p. 12.

THE PERSONALITY OF GOD

make room for both in one intelligence must lead before long to an explosive rupture.

These systems may be brought together summarily under the title of "idealistic Pantheism." Faith turns them down not because they are not good in part, and even excellent, but because their truth is spoiled by preponderant error. "That there is a truth in Pantheism," wrote Denney, "no one can question, a truth which poets, philosophers, and saints have all confessed; the difficulty is that it seems an all-devouring truth that leaves no room in the world for any other. God becomes so real in it that nothing else is real—not the intellect nor the conscience of man, not the difference between truth and falsehood, or between right and wrong. Instead of yielding a morality which is independent of religion, it yields a religion in which morality is engulfed and disappears. The Gospel offers us salvation in Christ; but instead of being saved in Christ, the pantheist is lost in God." To authentic Pantheism, God and the phenomenal cosmos are two names for one thing; but the Christian is sure that whatever God may be, He is not just the world. He is not even the soul of the world. Soul we mean as something limited by its body; but God as Christian faith conceives Him is high and lifted up, ineffably transcending earth and heaven. The fact is, Pantheism is not strictly a religion at all, but a speculative creed; one proof being that there has never been such a thing as a pantheist Church. At bottom it is a parasitic form of thought, attaching itself as an atmosphere or colour-tone to different species of philosophy but apparently incapable of independent life. One acid test of religious doctrines is the question: Would this tenet, if accepted seriously, go to sustain a community of redeemed men? Judged by this standard, Pantheism fails.

What better view can be put in its place? Surely we must emphasize the presence in God, in a real sense, of each of the three elements to be found in the inner spiritual life of man—knowledge, feeling, will. " In a real sense," I say; for no careful thinker would argue that when we call God a " mind," we mean that He is mind in precisely the same way as ourselves; but we do mean that we get infinitely nearer the truth when we speak of God's intelligence, will, and goodness than when we refuse to speak of these things and take our descriptive terms from the realm of physical nature. And yet it is not enough to single out any one of these three terms, and designate God as (for example) simply Knowledge or Intelligence. God conceived solely as Universal Thinker is not yet invested with true personality; and the history of metaphysical speculation shows how fatally easy on that hypothesis it is to press exclusively His immanence in the world, and let transcendence go by the board. All we are then in a position to affirm is God as contemplating the universe, or as sustaining by His dynamic thought the relationships of one thing to another;

THE PERSONALITY OF GOD

but we lose the right to say anything about a Divine centre of activity and enjoyment, such as is essential for the reality of what can truly be called a Self. In particular, the warmth and colour of specifically personal life disappear if no place is found for love, blessedness, joy, for all that might make God the home of ineffably profound desire and satisfaction—such desire as that for fellowship with His wayward children, or satisfaction over their return in faith and longing to His bosom. Theism, it is clear, has here insoluble problems on its hands so long as it conceives God as without a "heart," and declines to make room for what in the New Testament is a commonplace of religion.

Similarly, the presence of activity and will in the Divine life must be emphasized. Apart from will, the independent personal reality of God can hardly be more than a name. Deprive the person of power over himself; exclude the element of self-determination and self-direction; and at once there vanish all unity, continuity, spiritual persistence, for nothing is left but a seething mass of random impulses. It is especially in his purposes, not in the ideas and sensations that flit through his mind, that a man's authentic selfhood and character take shape and find outlet. Not otherwise can we conceive of God. There too we must think intelligent will as the centre of being. It is in His conscious purpose, activity, self-impulsion that God most absolutely lives a life incommunicably His own.

Great names, it is true, can be quoted on the

THE CHRISTIAN APPREHENSION OF GOD

other side. Aristotle, whose influence has too often operated in theology when men would have done better to follow Scripture, fixed upon theoretical excellence as the excellence proper to man, with the result that he placed the essence also of God in His intellectual being, and defined Him as "thought thinking upon itself." But if we have to choose between finding the inmost reality of Godhead in self-absorbed contemplation and finding it in an almighty loving Will that pours itself forth for the needy, no Christian is likely to hesitate. What we have discovered of God in Christ settles the point once for all; and a clear decision here will also decide some other points of first-rank importance, such as the possibility of forgiveness or the prospect of a blessed life after death. Thus the being we ascribe to God is in no sense indeterminate or religiously unmeaning; rather it is such a being as has created the specifically Christian faith. In Jesus we are in contact with a Divine Moral Self, with a God who takes sides, who stands for right and against wrong, in whom the deepest and constitutive reality is not pure thought or absolute knowledge but Personality constituted by infinite Holy Love. And there, in that holy redeeming Love which has touched and blessed us in Christ, giving us to know with perfect assurance that we are in contact with the last and highest reality in the universe—*there* is the crucial fact constraining us to say that God is personal. He is our Saviour, therefore we behold in Him One who knows and wills and loves.

THE PERSONALITY OF GOD

As it happens, the conception of the Divine personality has occasionally suffered even at the hands of Christian thinkers. We need not at present dwell upon the dreary metaphysical abstractions which some patristic and medieval writers were apt, in theoretical moments, to substitute for the Father of our Lord Jesus Christ. Not that the mistake is a purely ancient one. Some thinkers even in the nineteenth century have lapsed into an unfortunate ambiguity. Their argument follows, usually, a familiar and beaten track. Biedermann and Schweizer, for instance, urge that by intrinsic nature personality is something that grows; it is, in other words, not accidentally but essentially finite. This finite quality they find to be present universally in human personalities; and they infer, fallaciously as we shall see, that it is intrinsic to personality as such. Thus personality is in contradiction to the very idea of an infinite God. Even so warm-hearted a Christian as Schleiermacher yielded so far to the pantheistic influences of his age as to lean, at all events in his early writings, to the view that in itself religious feeling has no great concern in the question whether God is personal or not. Belief in a personal God, he declares, does not necessarily imply true piety, nor does disbelief in a personal God necessarily exclude it. This of course was tantamount to saying that the idea in question was one which the Christian mind can take or leave at will; the character of faith need not gain or suffer either way.

THE CHRISTIAN APPREHENSION OF GOD

But it was Strauss, author of the famous *Life of Jesus* (1835), who gave classical shape to this objection to the thought of Divine personality. He may be said to approach Christian theology in the spirit of the undertaker, engaged in burying what is dead. In a book on the Christian faith, published in 1840—a book of which it has been remarked that it resembles a theology only as a cemetery does a city—he takes up one by one the doctrines of the faith, with the object of showing that when you strain out every element derived from Scripture or vivid religious experience, then submit the whole to the ordeal of a rigorous historical criticism, nothing in the end is left but a faded residuum of speculative Pantheism. And it cannot be doubted that on these terms the idea of personality in its Divine reference is bound to fare badly. It does. He starts with a not too promising definition, which, so far from hiding its hard negation under a beautiful robe of words, puts it with a stark vigour. "Personality," he writes, " is the selfhood which shuts itself up against everything else, so as to exclude it ; the Absolute, on the other hand, is the All-comprehensive, the Unlimited, which excludes nothing at all except just that exclusiveness which attaches to the idea of personality."[1] Strauss is clearly of

[1] In a way this recalls the famous definition of a crab offered in an " oral " to the effect that it was a red fish that walked backwards, the examiner commenting that as a definition it was not so bad, except that a crab was not a fish, was not red, and did not walk backwards.

THE PERSONALITY OF GOD

opinion that personality and the like are conceptions applicable only to finite things, and that to transfer them to an Infinite or Universal Reality is to change their meaning. To be a person is perforce to be finite, because in order to exist and develop a self must have over against it a not-self through collision with which it comes to self-consciousness—a foil to provoke it, as it were, into independent being, just as the eye must be confronted by luminous objects, other than itself, if it is to see. Hence the Absolute, or God, which embraces all things, and therefore can have nothing over against it since everything is already within it, is not a Self or a person.

This argument, however, will only convince those who agree that Strauss's initial definition of personality is sound. For him it consists in exclusiveness as such; to be a self is to bar out everything and everybody from the citadel of one's own being, so that a group of persons can be best illustrated by a heap of pebbles, each of which is wholly outside all the rest. But surely it is the paradox of personality—a paradox we have simply to accept from life—that while each self does have a centre of its own which no other can occupy, and which enables each person to enjoy a private world of thoughts and feelings which are peculiarly his and no one else's, yet it is also true that just because we are persons we can transcend our isolation, and enter into the lives of other people. We do thus enter, in some degree, when we speak to them or understand

THE CHRISTIAN APPREHENSION OF GOD

their speech to us; we do it, still more profoundly, when we and they love each other. In short, the best modern thought is disposed to rank inclusiveness as a more important quality of personal being than exclusiveness as such. In the second place, a Christian will be slow to grant the assumption, on which Strauss's argument hangs, that the God he believes in is such an Absolute as contains everything, even our evil desires, as part of Himself. If then we disagree with Strauss about the meaning both of personality and of God, it need not greatly trouble us to find him laying down that the two ideas are incompatible.

The best-known reply to Strauss from the philosophic side was that of Lotze. He points out that it will not do simply to transfer to God what in reality are human defects. *We* are persons, indubitably; but we are persons in what may be styled a second-rate fashion. It is perfectly true that for the evocation of our conscious selfhood we have to be acted upon by external stimuli; we realize our self, that is, only through awareness of difference between ourselves and the surrounding world. So far good: but here we may perhaps go one step beyond Lotze. We may grant that human beings do become conscious of their own personality through touching others, and that if you think away all that has been contributed to our life by the social body we belong to, very little worth mentioning will be left. We notice ourselves because our intercourse with others has led us to notice ourselves. But it

THE PERSONALITY OF GOD

is *we* who notice ourselves; the noticing is not done for us, and it is not others who cause us to enjoy ourselves—to see and taste ourselves from the inside, so to speak—but the fact that we *are* selves. As Dalgairns has put it: "Because we arrive at the knowledge of our own personality through contact with that of others, it does not follow that personality itself is constituted by the sharp shock which comes of knocking our own self against another self. Things are determined by what they are, not by what they are not; an eagle is such because it is an eagle, not because it is not a lark." In other words, what awakes our self-consciousness does not for that reason make our self. And if personality is not even in our case produced by these foreign contacts and collisions, how much less with God!

But waiving this point, we may readily concur in Lotze's argument that while we are not self-sufficing, and do not contain within us the conditions of our own being or development, these marks of *human* personality cannot be carried over to God. He can both be personal, and know Himself as such, without having a not-self over against Him, in other words without being finite. It is logically fallacious to argue from defects in our personality to personality as such. To take an analogy, two centuries ago the prerogative of the Crown might have been held to be essential to the British Constitution, whereas as then exercised it was a defect, for it impeded the free expression of the nation's will. So, said Lotze,

THE CHRISTIAN APPREHENSION OF GOD

the particular form assumed by personal life in us does not fix what it may be elsewhere. It would be a contradiction to call God an evil being; it is no contradiction to call Him a personal being. And if we are told that limitations as such are unworthy of God, let us ask a plain question. Which limits God more—to say that He does have the capacity for fellowship, which is what personality is, or to say that He does *not* have it?[1]

All this is enough to show how superfluous the fear is that no philosophical reply can be made to philosophical objections. Much, however, may also be done in a positive way to state, and, by

[1] After writing out the argument given above, I was glad to find the following confirmation of its main drift in a recent essay by Professor John Macmurray. "The more universal," he writes, "a person becomes in his self-transcendence, the more unique does he become in his individuality. There is therefore no ground for hesitation in ascribing personality to God. Absolute personality, in terms of our analysis, must involve absolute universality and absolute individuality at once, each of these qualities being the condition of the other. The immanence of God is not at war with His transcendence. These are two aspects of the one fact. The transcendence of God is His unique individuality; His immanence is His absolute universality; and these are therefore not peculiar characteristics of Deity, but the fundamental characteristics of all personality carried to their infinite limit. What is human love but the immanence of one human personality in another? Yet it does no violence to the unique individuality, the transcendence, of either. . . . The idea that the supreme reality is an infinite personality is not self-contradictory, unless personality is conceived upon a false analogy with the individuality of non-rational or unconscious forms of being" (*Adventure*, edited by B. H. Streeter, pp. 193-4)

THE PERSONALITY OF GOD

stating, to defend the Christian belief in this matter. Thus it may be pointed out that self-conscious life is the highest type of reality with which we are acquainted, and most philosophers probably would agree that the fundamental principle of knowledge is interpretation by means of the highest category within our reach. Now when we contemplate the Spiritual Power that touches and moves us in Christ, and call in the loftiest interpretative conception at our disposal, we *must* call God a Self or Mind, if we are not to call Him something lower. And in this connexion it needs to be said emphatically that personality is no mere negative idea, diluting and reducing, as it were, the energy or range of life. On the contrary, it is affirmative and dynamic in a degree elsewhere unknown; it is intensely and uniquely positive, and so far from confining life is, when complete, a note of the highest level to which Being can attain. It is the power of spirit over itself, and this power may be finite or infinite. In us of course it is finite, since we do not create our own nature; we receive it, and never gain more than partial control over it. But in God, who is the ground of His own being, it is infinite, perfect, absolute.

Furthermore, personality is the only form in which we can think spiritual being as possessed of concrete existence. That is not an idiosyncrasy or weakness of religious thought, which a deeper philosophy is able to detect and throw off. The metaphysical reasons for preferring personal to

THE CHRISTIAN APPREHENSION OF GOD

impersonal names for the Supreme Reality are as true and cogent as the religious reasons for doing the same thing. But at present we are dealing with religion. And it is a remarkable indication of this inability of the religious mind, when it takes God seriously, to conceive Him otherwise than as personal, that men pray even when their theoretical idea of God is not such as would justify prayer, *e.g.* in fetishistic or animistic faiths. Over and over again the notion of the " supra-personal " has been called in to ease the difficulty ; but on analysis it has invariably turned out that " supra-personal," in the actual working of thought or imagination, becomes equivalent to " infra-personal," just as people of an extreme virtue who have grown superior to love for their own family are apt to be devoid of love altogether. The superman, as Nietzsche pictured him, is lower than man as we know him now ; and the supra-personal God is lower than personal, not higher. Take, for example, the idea of the Divine power. There are just two possible sources from which imaginative symbols may be drawn by which to represent it—the blind forces of Nature, and the self-conscious human will. Is God's power like an electric current or is it like the activity of a good man ? We are compelled to choose between these, a point which is illustrated curiously in the course of Herbert Spencer's famous argument about religion. Readers of his books will remember how he came at last to speak of " the Infinite and Eternal Energy from which all things proceed,"

THE PERSONALITY OF GOD

and how it grew clear to him that as a description this was scarcely adequate. He therefore went on to describe it as a force analogous to our own will. Not only so, unknowable though it be, he next declared that " it stands towards our general conception of things, substantially as does the Creative Power asserted by theology." Still further, and most significant of all, he reached the final view that in us this Infinite Energy wells up in the form of consciousness. No wonder that John Fiske, an able American disciple, took the one remaining step and definitely argued for Theism. With regard to the personality of God, indeed, while Spencer professed to hold a position of pure agnosticism, he went so far as to say that if personality is inadmissible as a predicate of the Absolute, we must affirm what is higher than personal, not something lower. That is a suggestion to which we may well listen with respect.

Perhaps we may say more than that. Does not Spencer give us a salutary reminder of the limits even of our best thoughts of God ? After all, personality in us is more an analogy than an exact copy of the spiritual being we ascribe to God ; and, as Canon Streeter has said, " In speaking of God as personal, we are expanding the idea of personality to meet this special case." The life He possesses is, to put it so, infinitely further up and further on in the line on which we ourselves stand. So much is vouched for by the great converse principle laid down in Scripture, that man is made in God's image. Let the line of ethical selfhood on which we are placed be prolonged, and at some incalculably higher point we must think of the selfhood of God as existing with ineffable perfectness. "He," not "It," is the word we rightly use to throw out our minds at the absolute object. And thus, to express the whole truth of which faith is aware, we must strive to balance together these two convictions: first, that personality in Him utterly transcends ours, being inexpressibly higher, richer, more living than its earthly type, and secondly, that none the less to deny Him personality would be infinitely farther from the truth than to affirm it in the properly expanded sense. Of our thoughts concerning the spiritual being of God it is supremely true that *omnia exeunt in mysterium*—unfathomableness is the end of all.

But to descend from these altitudes, let us ask: What does the personality of God signify for the religious man? What does it count for in Christian faith that overcomes the world? The best answer comes from the Bible. There we find no strictly doctrinal reasonings on the subject, yet unquestionably we find the thing. We find it in a great recurrent Bible phrase: "the living God." The Psalmist writes, "my heart and my flesh crieth out for the living God,"[1] and Jeremiah declares that "the Lord is the living God and an everlasting King."[2] As we have seen, when we

[1] Ps. lxxxiv. 2.   [2] Jer. x. 10.

THE PERSONALITY OF GOD

speak of the Divine personality, we are thinking of an infinitely rich and mobile spiritual form of being that inwardly enjoys its own blessedness and ponders its own vast purpose and, outwardly, reacts with sensitive awareness on human life in mercy and judgment; and what the words "the living God" convey is precisely this mobility, sensitiveness, conscious thought and activity. In Scripture, God is known to be living, that is personal, by His wondrous deeds.

Thus if we would grasp the being of God as measurelessly personal in character, the Bible advises us, not to close our eyes and retreat into our inner mind, which is the purely mystic way, nor to analyse ideas, which is the method of *a priori* rationalism; but to behold great facts which form part of the human history we ourselves inhabit, and let their meaning take possession of us. The apprehension of the living God came to prophetic believers of the Old and New Testaments from the impact of definite events laden with truth concerning the Unseen, truth which a higher Spirit than their own enabled them to appropriate inwardly. When this clue has been lost, or put aside as having exhausted its value, the difficulty of keeping hold upon the Divine personality is all but insuperable.

In any case, it was in these terms that the Apostles proclaimed their gospel. They preached, as St Peter affirms, " the mighty works of God."[1] They took it as their chief task to let men know

[1] Acts ii. 11.

THE CHRISTIAN APPREHENSION OF GOD

what the living God has done, is doing, and will yet do. They bore witness to the coming and going of Jesus Christ, and these known facts they left to make their own impression. Let them only be understood, and they would instil their lesson as to who and what God is. The human word could not be spoken till the revealing act had been done. Thus the element in the apostolic message that called out faith and did real work, was passionate testimony to actual events.

To-day the effective missionary follows the same plan. And if all other tests of religious truth gave out, we might perhaps fall back confidently on this negative one, that the message which does not evangelize, the view of Christianity which fails to convert, abroad or at home, cannot be true. Whatever else it may be, it emphatically is not the power of God unto salvation. But proclamation of the mighty works of God is still—so the life-work of missionaries who live their truth as well as teach it makes certain—the one effectual means by which non-Christian minds can be given the clear thought of God as a personal Father. What tells with liberating and revolutionary power is not so much explanation as presentation. The learners, slowly yet unfailingly, rise by the ladder of history to a redeeming conviction of the personal being of God, with whom they can have the communion of loved and pardoned children.

In this respect they are very like ourselves. In his *Life of Carlyle*, Froude reports a conversation

THE PERSONALITY OF GOD

that occurred not long before Carlyle's death. "I said to him that I could only believe in a God which did something. With a cry of pain, which I shall never forget, he said, 'He does nothing.'" That cry came from the deep instinct that faith can only be created and sustained by the deeds of God, and that Deity which said nothing and did nothing could not be apprehended as personally alive.

Thus we can give a conclusive reason for affirming the personality of God. We can say: it is in this character He encounters us in Christ, the great Doer of redeeming things. No other conception enables us to attach a positive meaning to the purposes, thoughts, and feelings He has manifested in His Son. The voice that speaks in conscience, telling of sin and accountability, we know without reasoning to be the voice of a person; so too the voice of infinite love, declaring that our sin is pardoned and that at once, without waiting to become any better, we may come home to God, is a personal voice or it is nothing but a dream. "The love of God loses all meaning for the heart, if He ceases to be a person to the mind."[1]

---

[1] D. W. Forrest, *The Authority of Christ*, p. 47.

CHAPTER VI

THE HOLINESS OF GOD

The Christian apprehension of God, which we are trying to elucidate, is a topic so illimitable in scope and difficulty that we must be satisfied to select, with what wisdom we may, those aspects of the theme which by common consent are primary. In the last chapter we tried to think out the problem of the Divine personality. In the next three chapters attention will be called to those characteristics—or, as they are often called, attributes—of God which the Christian mind has always felt to be of crucial moment : His holiness, His love, His sovereignty.

The proposal to define God may well appear symptomatic of irreverence. He is the Infinite One, and to define is in logic to make Him finite, or has a look of that. " Canst thou find out the Almighty unto perfection ? " is a warning word from the past. Yet, as we have seen, some working conception of God we must have, some outline that controls our thinking and ensures that what we say has a real connexion with the facts of religious life. Let us start with the following first sketch of a definition, used for clearness and brevity but with our eyes wide open to its inadequacy : God is the Absolute Personality in whom Holiness, Love, and Power are perfect and are one. I say the " Personality " capable of

THE HOLINESS OF GOD

being described thus, but I say so without prejudice to the further interpretation of that word which might come from reflection on the Divine life of Christ, and on the Holy Spirit. It is conceivable, that is to say, that if we think out and think through the notion of self-existent Deity, we may eventually discover that a barely monistic conception of it breaks down. We may be led to believe, for example, that God cannot intelligibly be imaged as Eternal Love unless we go on to project into the Godhead the eternal distinction between infinite and unbeginning Love and its no less infinite and unbeginning Object. It is not incredible that, as it has been put, "within His unique Being there must for ever be something which is the counterpart of that living interaction of subject and object, that communing of soul with soul in love, which to us is possible only in a society of persons and a universe of things." But this baffling problem, known as the doctrine of the Trinity, we here put on one side. At this point we need only say that no Trinitarian definitions can be accepted which conflict with the believing certainty that God is personal. If Trinitarianism meant tritheism, *i.e.* belief in three Gods, all will agree it would be unchristian.

We have described God as "the Absolute Personality in whom Holiness, Love, and Power are perfect and are one." Looking closely at this, we can make out that here there are, speaking broadly, two distinguishable sides. One side is for modern thought represented by the words holiness and love, the other by the word power. And for the fully Christian thought of God *both* are essential. The differentia of God as Christ revealed Him lies in their coalescence, their sheerly indissoluble unity. When a Christian says " God," he does not mean " Holy Love " simply ; he means absolute or almighty holy love ; and the term almighty stands for a vital feature apart from which God would not be God. Christianity was the first religion to affirm unconditionally that God is love, but in making this affirmation it in no sense implied that He is love alone, and that once this supreme ethical level of conception had been reached, every other attribute might safely be ignored. The idea of absoluteness or omnipotence was presupposed, even when not stated expressly. But still less does almightiness exhaust what Christians mean by God. In mere power as such, whatever its magnitude, there is nothing to evoke the worship of a moral being or to win the free homage of conscience. Omnipotence, divorced from moral character, lapses into arbitrary and unmotived force. God, then, is both these things in a living unity—holy love and absolute power.

But further, these two aspects do not combine with each other by any logical necessity. This is a point of some importance. Love when analysed does not yield power as one of its intrinsic elements, nor does power yield love. After all it is only as believers that we are certain of their unity in God ; our insight into their oneness in Him is

THE HOLINESS OF GOD

the insight not of speculation but of faith. Holy love, so far as I can see, is not incapable of being conceived apart from power on an absolute scale. Yet it belongs to the special character of the highest religion that throughout the ages it has so wonderfully viewed this unity of holy love and power in God as spiritually self-evident. It takes the unity for granted; in more technical terms, that unity is for the religious mind a matter of *a priori* knowledge. In Otto's words, written from the standpoint of religion, "This is the criterion of all *a priori* knowledge, namely, that so soon as an assertion has been clearly expressed and understood, knowledge of its truth comes into the mind with the certitude of first-hand insight."[1] Faith intuitively perceives not only that there is holy love in God, but also that this holy love has a mode of being in virtue of which it is expressed in the universe and rules transcendently over all finite things for the realization of its glorious purpose. All that is in God is ethically qualified, but not all can be stated in purely ethical terms.

Thus we come up against one feature of the thought of God concerning which Christian thinkers in recent years have had much to say, viz., the presence in it of difficult inward tensions. These tensions make it impossible for faith to hold its knowledge of God with quiet or detached unconcern, as we might some piece of scientific information; to hold it at all, we must constantly be winning it anew, for its internal difficulties

[1] *The Idea of the Holy*, p. 141.

THE CHRISTIAN APPREHENSION OF GOD

give us no rest. Every one feels that at first glance the world does not look like a place governed by a God who is *both* loving and almighty. If that is His nature, where do the grief and the sin come from ? An all-powerful God (we tend to say), uninfluenced by love or influenced only in a slight degree, might have made this world; or if He *is* loving, the obstacles have been too much for His power. Another severe tension is that between His love and His holiness. If a loving God receives sinners, does not a holy God repel them ; if, as holy, He reacts with displeasure against sin, can He love the sinful ? To the logical understanding it appears as if the only way out were to deny one side of the tension and assert the other. To faith, on the other hand, it is clear that both sides must be asserted unconditionally. As Christians, we cannot believe in a God who is only loving or holy or almighty up to a point. Absoluteness is the mark of His being. But at least the fact that we are unable to allay these painful tensions is proof of one thing; it is proof that God, as Christians worship Him, is unsearchable. He is not unknowable, for in Christ we have seen His faithful and unchanging love ; but in His nature there is unfathomable mystery. If in some respects this consideration weighs upon faith as a burden, in others it is an exalting and even triumphant thought. Could One in whom there was no mystery content our infinite nature ? Surely it is evident that a God perfectly transparent for human reason would be God no longer.

THE HOLINESS OF GOD

In this chapter we are studying the Holiness of God. Twenty years ago, a discussion of this topic would largely have been concentrated on the moral perfection and purity which, for our minds, the word holiness connotes. Such perfection and purity is indeed part of its meaning, so that this distribution of emphasis would have been natural enough. To-day, however, largely owing to Otto's striking book *The Idea of the Holy*, the position has changed. Otto has afresh made us feel that an exclusively moral conception of God is not quite in focus, and that the Biblical conception of holiness, properly understood, stands for all in God's being that transcends reason in the narrower sense, all that towers up in infinite sublimity over man and the world. The holy is a category—*i.e.* a fundamental conception—by itself, just as the good or the beautiful is; it cannot be derived from any other idea, or grown out of it, any more than the idea of the moral can be grown out of the useful, or the beautiful out of the pleasant. Holiness, in short, is not (if the Bible is any guide) to be taken in a simply or exclusively ethical sense, but has a nature of its own; it is not reducible to elements which do not already contain its distinctive quality. I am tempted to call it " indefinable." Yet it is not on that account meaningless, for, to take a rough but not wholly unfit analogy, although I cannot define " blue " or " sweet," in the sense of finding a simpler explanation of them than themselves, I know quite well what these words mean.

Similarly, impalpable as "holiness" may be, it can be talked about, and statements about the holiness of God can be made which the devout understand perfectly. Failure to allow for this special quality has spoiled many an otherwise hopeful book on religion. If we reflect carefully upon what happens in our minds when we are in a specifically *reverent* mood, we can make out that reverence is not compounded merely of things like gratitude, trust, love, or confidence; for all these we might feel towards an exceptionally good man. There is something over and above; there is an awareness of the Holy One. To use a natural expression, we are "solemnized." We are filled with awe, with what the apostle calls "godly fear," as we listen to the great words: "Holy, Holy, Holy, is the Lord of Hosts; the whole earth is full of his glory."[1]

This aspect of the Divine holiness, this supernal grandeur in the Holy One that brings us through a feeling of creaturehood to sink in nothingness before His majesty, is of course especially familiar in the Old Testament. "Holy," in that earlier time, was at first virtually equivalent to "Divine." "When God is described as the Holy One in the Old Testament," it has been said, "it is generally with the purpose of withdrawing Him from some presumption of men upon His majesty or of negativing their unworthy thoughts of Him."[2] As holy, God is separate from man in his frailty

[1] Isa. vi. 3.
[2] G. A. Smith, *The Book of Isaiah*, Vol. I, p. 64.

THE HOLINESS OF GOD

and fugitiveness. When we try to put in words what His holiness means, terms like unapproachable, sublime, exalted, infinite rise in the mind. There is a supernatural and more-than-rational background to the idea; it is akin to the blinding *glory* of the Lord which flashed on the prophet's soul in the 6th chapter of Isaiah. The holy is " sacred " in contrast to " profane." As we shall see, this mysterious and awe-creating aspect of holiness is never alone, or by itself, in the religion of the Old Testament; always it is being progressively shot through and coloured by moral elements. But it is there; and Otto has opened our eyes freshly to the fact that it remains there even in the New Testament. Think, for example, of Jesus' message concerning the Kingdom of God. That was no poetic idyll. On the contrary, there is something in it which awakens a solemn awe, for " the Kingdom " is specifically Divine; it is a supernatural reality, belonging to another realm than ours, a gift from above that does not come out of the world but comes into it. How the evangelists often strike the note of wonder! The Heavenly Father, whose gift the Kingdom is, is not less sacred or unfathomable for Jesus than He is for the faith of the prophets, but more so; more than ever He is the Lord high and lifted up. He is distinct from man; it is still true that " my ways are higher than your ways, and my thoughts than your thoughts."[1] Not that Jesus

[1] Isa. lv. 9.

merely revealed God as the Holy One, thus reiterating Israel's faith; what He taught, and what gives His revelation its literally boundless import, is the all but unbelievable paradox that *the Holy One is our Father*. The gospel we owe to Christ, the gospel that multitudes in their agony have heard and rejoiced in as they laid their ear close to the New Testament, is the truth that the Holy God receives sinners. He who dwells in light that no man can approach unto, is ours in Jesus. The light of that awful holiness hangs over the garden of Gethsemane, where in the hour of His visitation Christ, as we read in Hebrews, " offered up prayers and supplications with strong crying and tears unto him that was able to save him from death, and was heard in that he feared."[1]

Yet even in the Old Testament this is not the whole truth regarding the holiness of God. If it means primarily that vast "wholly other" sublimity which makes God distinct from man and evokes a feeling of peculiar awe—that unique dread or thrill which Otto has taught us to call "numinous"—it more and more comes also to mean moral purity and intolerance of sin. Passages may easily be found in the prophets which lay stress firmly on the ethical character of holiness. It is to the holiness of God that Hosea relates His compassion: " I will not return to destroy Ephraim: for I am God and not man; the Holy One in the midst of thee."[2] Isaiah conceives

[1] Heb. v. 7. [2] Hos. xi. 9.

THE HOLINESS OF GOD

God's holiness as being demonstrated by the righteousness of His action: "The Lord of hosts is exalted in judgment, and God the Holy One is sanctified in righteousness."[1] Thus it is an idea quite familiar to the prophets that the Divine holiness is an utter sublimity based or rooted in moral perfection.

This line of teaching, as we might anticipate, is given a larger prominence in the New Testament. Not that passages are numerous in which the epithet is applied to God directly; they are in fact curiously few, hardly more than Jesus' address "Holy Father,"[2] and the words of 1 Peter: "Like as he which called you is holy, be ye yourselves also holy in all manner of living."[3] Christ also is spoken of as "the Holy One" and the Divine Spirit is "Holy Spirit." But everywhere the strain of prophetic thought which pointed to God's ethical purity and absolute hostility to sin is carried on in a deepened form. His holiness has immediate relations to right and wrong in human life. Moral experience has once for all taken a central place in the knowledge of God, so much so that a modern tendency to restrict the Divine holiness to a moral significance might seem to have a great deal to say for itself. Yet the counter-stroke must follow, if we are to keep the balance of truth: even in the New Testament the awe-inspiring element remains, and remains as vital. " Our God is a consuming

[1] Isa. v. 16.   [2] John xvii. 11.   [3] 1 Pet. i. 15.

fire,"[1] we read in Hebrews; He dwells "in light unapproachable"[2] is another phrase with its supernatural suggestion. God, as holy, is separate from man and from his sin. Even in the presence of Jesus this impression lives on. His loftiness brings awe upon those around Him; not only do those who seek to arrest Him go backward and fall to the ground, but of the disciples too we read that as they followed the lonely Figure on His way to Jerusalem, "they were afraid."[3] Jesus too is holy, in the full profound sense of the word—not only, as has been said, "separate from sinners, but distinct from the saints."

As we look back, it is clear that the changes in the felt meaning of holiness are of crucial import for the history of religion. In Dr Glover's words, "The term 'holy,' if we could trace it through all the successive suggestions, would be a tell-tale word, as it moved from the physical and all but irrational onward through the moral to the spiritual." There are religions which for Christian thought lapse at once to an inferior plane in virtue of their defects at this point. Ancient Hinduism, for example, ascribed all sorts of qualities in their highest power to Brahman, but nowhere did it declare that Brahman is holy or righteous.

If then God be moral perfection and purity, the moral law alive and transcendent over the world, the old dilemma which logic seemed to

[1] Heb. xii. 29. [2] 1 Tim. vi. 16. [3] Mark x. 32.

THE HOLINESS OF GOD

force upon the thinker is no longer an embarrassment. It ran something like this: Is the good good because God wills it, or does He will it because it is good in itself and by its own right? Here obviously the assumption is that good and God can be separated in thought, so that their relations to each other may become a matter of dispute and we have to find reasons for uniting them. But the difficulty vanishes, once the idea of God has been completely moralized. God does will the good, for invariably He acts in conformity with His intrinsic nature; and yet, just as truly, good is not in any sense an entity or power outside God, or over Him, with which even He has to come to terms. Only in Him, indeed, has the good utterly real existence; apart from God, and those to whom God communicates His life, goodness is no more than an abstract noun.

In recent times, a vivacious debate sprang up round the subject of this chapter, owing largely to Ritschl's proposal to drop the conception of the Divine holiness altogether out of Christian theology, on the ground that its interests are sufficiently provided for by a proper interpretation of the Divine love. "In its Old Testament sense," he writes, "it is for various reasons not valid in Christianity, while its use in the New Testament is obscure."[1] What was in his mind is plain. He had learned from his friend Diestel that in the Old Testament holiness does not in the first instance mean ethical per-

[1] *Justification and Reconciliation* (English translation), p. 274.

fection; it means, as we have seen, that in God which is absolute, supramundane, and surpassing all the measures of human reason. This offended Ritschl's deeply ethical temper; and, since the moral significance of Christianity counted for everything with him, he drew the inference that " holiness," in that extra-moral sense, is incongruous with the Divine love revealed in Christ. What he failed to see is that even within the Old Testament the holiness of God comes to embrace also moral goodness. It is ultimately the living conjunction of the absolutely good and the sacrosanct.

However this may be, and whatever the limitations of Ritschl's insight, the debate he set on foot had one result of prime importance. People woke up anew to the subduing fact that the holiness of God, as manifest in Jesus, is a self-imparting quality. The Bible will not hear of our confining it strictly to the nature of God Himself, as if it were not perpetually striving to convey itself to His frail and polluted children. Or, to put it otherwise, the Divine holiness has a redemptive and not merely a condemnatory aspect; in the light of Jesus, we see it to be self-bestowing. Holy love—and holiness as intrinsically as love is constitutive of the Ultimate Reality we name God—is the fount of all salvation. The opposition to sin which is central to its meaning is an opposition exhibited at least as much in forgiveness as in judgment. This is a point which is illustrated with special force and

THE HOLINESS OF GOD

beauty in the Old Testament. In the prophetic writings, the holiness of God, instead of merely repelling and overwhelming the sinful, frequently becomes the very fact to which the believer fastens his confidence. " Thou art holy, O thou that inhabitest the praises of Israel. Our fathers trusted in thee: they trusted, and thou didst deliver them ";[1] and again, " As for our Redeemer, the Lord of Hosts is his name, the Holy One of Israel." [2] But the same profound and consoling thought is expressed by Jesus' parting words as recorded in the Fourth Gospel : " Holy Father, keep through thine own name those whom thou hast given me." [3] It is as *holy* that God redeems and keeps men.

This of course is an aspect of truth with a direct bearing on what has been called Atonement, but is better called Reconciliation. Alike in theory and in preaching the assumption has too often been made that whatever the sinful may rightly hope for from God's mercy, from His holiness they can hope for nothing. The spotless and transcendent purity of God must of necessity repel and exclude the man who has stained himself with evil. Even this is significant of a great and solemn truth, for it has been justly said that the proclamation of God's love can scarcely be understood, except by those who have first been awed by the holiness of God. None the less, a view

[1] Ps. xxii. 3-4.
[2] Isa. xlvii. 4 ; cf. xli. 14, xlviii. 17, xlix. 7, liv. 5.
[3] John xvii. 11.

of that kind has often rested on a conception of holiness in God as something exclusively formidable and menacing. M'Leod Campbell—the greatest of all Scottish theologians, to whom perhaps more than to any other single mind we to-day owe a spiritual interpretation of the central Christian ideas—guides us better here. He is aware of the double meaning of holiness as a Divine quality, and fully allows for it. But he is also aware that for those who have beheld God in Christ, the partition between love and holiness has broken down and the nature of each of them has diffused through the whole. " In one view," he writes, " the holiness of God repels the sinner, and would banish him to outer darkness, because of its repugnance to sin. In another it is pained by the continued existence of sin and unholiness, and must desire that the sinner should cease to be sinful. So that the sinner, conceived as awakening to the consciousness of his own evil state, and saying to himself, " By sin I have destroyed myself. Is there yet hope for me in God ? " should hear an encouraging answer, not only from the love and mercy of God, but also from His very holiness."[1]

It is clear that in apprehending the holiness of God we are in contact with paradox. When it first breaks upon us, we are conscious of a certain suspense or hesitation ; there is a sense of being checked, or baffled, or even stupefied, or possibly even repelled or threatened, as though something

[1] *The Nature of the Atonement* (6th edition), p. 26.

THE HOLINESS OF GOD

were affecting us that we could not receive, or grasp, or stand up to. An experience of God so great has been conveyed that it throws the mind as it were off its balance and produces a feeling of sheer inability to grapple with what has been presented. And yet behind this consciousness of tension and irreconcilability of contrasted aspects, there is a quite definite and unified *conviction*—viz., that God is encountering us in grace. Grace means that in His loving self-bestowal His severity is absorbed, yet does not disappear. It is a stringent love, and by being less stringent God would become not more loving but less Divine. We can check our thought of the holiness of God by observing the holiness of Jesus. Here the same two-sided impression emerges. He was perfectly open-eyed about the evil in human life, and by being near Him men's eyes opened to its virulent presence in themselves. There is a dread incidental severity in the two interjected words, " if ye then, *being evil*, know how to give good gifts to your children."[1] His holiness burned with a scorching flame in which foul things were exposed and consumed. " He told me all things that ever I did,"[2] said one who had spent half an hour in His company. All this elicited in His associates the insight that they were unworthy to be in His presence. And yet that very holiness, by which they felt themselves judged, was seeking them from hour to hour. It was a condemning holiness; yes, but also it

[1] Matt. vii. 11.   [2] John iv. 29.

was a tender and merciful holiness, and it was essentially both. Precisely when men began to feel shame and to perceive the tragedy and hatefulness of their sin with sad-eyed clearness, just then it broke upon them that Jesus was their friend. St Peter sank down at His feet crying, "Depart from me, for I am a sinful man"; but Jesus in response would not depart or withdraw His comradeship from the stricken man; instead He said "Fear not," and kept Peter on beside Him.[1] His attitude was at once so stern and so kind, so gentle and so unrelenting, that through Him the redemptive holiness of God touched and blessed their lives, and gradually or in a flash their minds opened through Him to faith in the Father. We are accustomed in creed and prayer to say that Jesus Christ is the perfect revelation of God; but this soundest of generalizations we tend to construe too broadly, without much troubling to apply it in detail. There is no point in the Divine character on which we might more fitly bring it to bear than holiness. If we wish to know what *kind* of holiness is in God, let us look steadily at Jesus. Let us contemplate Him as He shames the bad, and welcomes the penitent, and stretches the hand of love down into the depths of guilt, and infallibly we shall learn what it signifies to name God "holy."

We have seen at an earlier point that the "righteousness" of God designates His pure

[1] Luke v. 8-10.

THE HOLINESS OF GOD

goodness in His dealings with men. He is righteous as being morally perfect in His government of the world. His rule over all things is self-consistent; it is all of a piece, and harmonious in the ultimate ethical sense. His character and His ways are wholly trustworthy; He is never wanting on His part, but true to His own nature and bent on pursuing a coherent purpose to its glorious end. Therefore, in a great word, we speak of Him as righteous.

Here two main aspects of truth engage us; at all events there are two on which we are bound to reflect with special care. If in virtue of His righteousness God sustains the moral order of the universe, or perhaps rather Himself *is* that moral order as a living reality, one illustration of this will be found in His punishment of sin. The religious consciousness, at least on the plane of Scripture, believes dimly or luminously in a God who, in the prophet Nahum's phrase, " will by no means clear the guilty."[1] As we shall see presently, this is a point round which difficulties gather. These difficulties bulked so largely in Ritschl's mind, that he positively suggested we should cut out the punitive aspect of the Divine righteousness, at all events when regarded as more than accidental. In his view, the righteousness of God is not merely in harmony with, but indistinguishable from, His grace. But most exegetes have felt, surely with justice, that it is no better than a *tour de force* to expel the element

[1] Verse 3, cap. i.

THE CHRISTIAN APPREHENSION OF GOD

of punitive righteousness from the Biblical thought of Divine action. To take only St Paul, that salient phrase, which occurs so often in Romans and may almost be said to form the subject of the Epistle, " the righteousness of God," whatever more it means, means in part at least that self-maintaining reaction of God's nature against moral evil which cannot but issue in active condemnation of it. Or again, can we believe that no basis exists in the character of God for the particular quality of the moral order which ensures that " whatsoever a man soweth, that shall he also reap " ?[1] And if there is such a basis, what could it be except His righteousness ?

Indeed, the conviction that none other than God Himself is behind the punishment of sin constitutes, for the Christian mind, the foundation of penal law in human society. Those who administer law fulfil a holy office, for they act—with whatever inevitable failure perfectly to achieve their end—in God's name. They are engaged in a cause by all odds higher than mere expediency, for it rests on the inviolable distinction of good and evil. This was in Hooker's mind, when he spoke in famous words of law " whose seat is the bosom of God, whose voice is the harmony of the world."

The disposition to say that to " punish " is unworthy of God has probably often arisen from the belief that the punishments in question are conceived in what is purely or predominantly

[1] Gal. vi. 7.

THE HOLINESS OF GOD

a hedonistic fashion, also that they attach themselves quite externally to the act or career on which they supervene. But this is caricature. If I say to another or to myself: Give the rein to base impulse, and even bodily you will reap as you have sown, but in addition you will forfeit peace of conscience, the respect of those you revere, and felt communion with God—if I say this, I am not preaching hedonism, nor am I threatening the trespasser with penalties intrinsically out of relation to the trespass. I am simply pointing to the constitution of things, which in some real degree registers the will of God. When the Psalmist wrote, " Before I was afflicted I went astray, but now I keep thy word,"[1] he was not guilty of a fantastic misinterpretation; he was putting in words what thousands know to be the truth.

We may demur to certain of Ritschl's negative findings; we cannot refuse his challenge to look deeper into the righteousness of God. He does seem to be right in contending that righteousness is inseparably bound up with grace. It is evident that the Western philosophical and juristic tradition—formulated in a classic way by Aristotle and given imposing practical shape in Roman Law—has too often misled religion into conceiving righteousness as a quality in God in virtue of which He treats each " exactly as he deserves " ; but when we try to relate this to His love, we fail utterly. For in this sense righteousness, to put

[1] Ps. cxix. 67.

it broadly, stands for two things. First, the distributive justice according to which each is encouraged to hope precisely for what he can claim, no less and no more; and secondly, the fact that justice, in punishing and rewarding, strikes an exact or approximately exact ratio between merit or demerit and reward or penalty. But observe what this means. It means that the conditions of an earthly State, and the laws which for its own ends it makes and enforces, have been chosen as the best analogy to God the Father's treatment of His children. Now it is of the first importance to observe that this does not cover even the finest things in earthly experience. No true parent ever dreams of treating his family by such a principle. Altogether apart from Christianity, we are never, any of us, dealt with " exactly as we deserve." What have we done to " deserve " that there should be such a thing as physical science, or the system of railway transport, or (to rise to a different level) the noble heritage of English poetry? These things we find here when we arrive at birth; we gain daily advantage from them; they are helps and ornaments of life, without which we should not know ourselves; but with their reality, or our share in their benefits and remissions, our merits have nothing to do. Thus, even in the wide and varied field of human civilization, we obtain freely more by far than our due. Our share of unearned increment is incalculable. In that case, it is unlikely—to use a mild expression—that the principle of dis-

THE HOLINESS OF GOD

tributive justice can be more than a clumsy index of God's ways with men. He must be far more than a scrupulously precise Dispenser of prizes to the good and inflictions to the bad.

Every idea of the righteousness of God is therefore to be repudiated (in view of Christ) from which no pathway can be found to the Divine love. In saying this, we are supported by the best teaching of prophets and apostles. To start from the circumference, let us recollect that in Scripture God is righteous not merely in bringing home his responsibility to the sinner, but in lifting up the oppressed and down-trodden. That idea entered the Old Testament mind through the conception of God as Judge, and it is easy to forget how noble the Hebrew thought of a judge is. It was his part to see right done to the weak; and thence the transition was simple to the insight that it is peculiarly worthy of God to succour all who are weakened and oppressed by sin. Whether or not the prophetic mind travelled by this road, at all events in Deutero-Isaiah we are full in view of great truth that the righteousness of God is a missionary attribute. By its nature, not accidentally, it strives to communicate itself. The moral order of the world is laden with redemption. A. B. Davidson has put this memorably. " The antithesis which in dogmatics[1] we are familiar with is a righteous or just God and *yet* a Saviour. The Old Testament puts it differently—a righteous God, and

[1] He ought to have said, *bad* dogmatics.

THE CHRISTIAN APPREHENSION OF GOD

therefore a Saviour. It is His own righteousness that causes Him to bring in righteousness."[1] There is here no opposition to grace. "There is no God else beside me, a just God and a Saviour; look unto me, and be ye saved, all the ends of the earth."[2] In one Psalm righteousness is actually put in contrast to judgment, *i.e.* to the very thing which technically brings it to expression: "Answer me in thy righteousness, and enter not into judgment with thy servant."[3] If God condemns, it is that He may save.

In the New Testament the same note sounds even more distinctly. The righteousness of God, as St Paul sets it forth in Romans, is the background of the Cross, and the Cross is the medium of salvation. The thought is perhaps put most strikingly of all in the Johannine verse: "If we confess our sins, he is faithful and righteous to forgive us our sins."[4] God forgives the penitent—this is the writer's meaning—for it would be out of harmony with all that He has revealed of His nature, supremely in Christ, were He not to pardon those who make confession. There is nothing here to enforce the principle by which theology has so often been wrongly guided, that men being sinners nothing is due to them from God. The Bible has obviously no difficulty in combining righteousness and love or grace as vitally related ideas, which in unity form the basis of salvation. There is promise for sinful

[1] *Old Testament Theology*, p. 144.
[2] Isa. xlv. 21-22.   [3] Ps. cxliii. 1-2.   [4] 1 John i. 9.

THE HOLINESS OF GOD

men, as they return to the Father, in that Father's very righteousness; they may with confidence cast themselves on the longing which has throbbed in God's heart from all eternity to impart what forms the glory and the blessedness of His own life.

If this be true, it also has a crucial bearing on the doctrine of Atonement. There has been a common tendency to speak of God's endeavour to reconcile men to Himself as if it implied a conflict or antithesis of attributes within His being—mercy and judgment striving together and each standing upon its rights. In sermons long ago I have myself heard imaginary dialogues as between these two, in which they stated their case alternately, justice demanding that the sinner should be cast into perdition, mercy that he should be pitied and redeemed. What lies behind this representation ? Why have men been led to speak thus of God ? Certainly not by accident. On the contrary, there is an inner law that compels the sinful to look upon God as a wrathful Judge. It is their penalty that the guilty must regard God so, and that His pardoning love is hidden from them by their overwhelming sense of His pure, unapproachable righteousness. Estrangement from the Father has this inevitable psychological result. And in one view, the service rendered by Christ to sinful men is to convince them that in God a forgiving grace obtains that is mightier than the justice before which they trembled. It is the anxious soul, the alarmed but not yet pacified conscience, that unavoidably conceives the righteousness of God as such that it *must* conflict with love. But from the standpoint of faith, His sternest righteousness is felt to be in harmony with love, its medium and instrument. That antinomy of the older time is one more consequence of failing to theologize solely from the angle of positive and specifically Christian faith. Each question must be raised and each must be answered exclusively in the light of the Gospel as trustful hearts receive it. The impressions of the " anxious inquirer " (to use an old-fashioned term) must in every case be replaced by the convictions of faith—the faith evoked and satisfied by Christ.

Yes: in all our thinking about the great righteousness of God, it is to the Christian conscience that we must listen—the conscience made sensitive and exacting by His inestimable love in Jesus. When we so listen, we are aware that He demands goodness from us and that He judges evil. He is the Power of Goodness over all things; in Him that perfection is not merely authoritative but mighty. Yet mark how greatly this His righteous character is fulfilled and crowned in the Gospel for a world of sin. His method of saving men through Christ, far from being the contradiction or reversal of His righteousness, is its utterly effective expression. His supreme moral power is for the first time having free course in His world, for the rightness of mind and heart which He demands from men He now freely bestows; He not merely convinces of evil, but

THE HOLINESS OF GOD

redeems us from it. Here righteousness moves hand in hand with perfect love. Whatever men's thoughts, it has ever been so. There has never been a time when God punished for punishment's sake, but at each stage the manifestation of His righteousness has opened the way by which love might enter, and the apprehension of His love in turn has enabled men, as nothing else could, to rise up and fulfil the challenge of His righteous will. Thus if it be understood for what it is, the grace we encounter in Jesus can never foster moral apathy within us. Rather it is the one incentive which, by delivering us triumphantly from self, can bring us to seek first the Kingdom of God and His righteousness.

The sense of God as holy and righteous informs Binney's noble lines :

> Eternal Light ! eternal Light !
> How pure the soul must be,
> When, placed within Thy searching sight,
> It shrinks not, but, with calm delight,
> Can live, and look on Thee !
>
> Oh, how shall I, whose native sphere
> Is dark, whose mind is dim,
> Before the Ineffable appear,
> And on my naked spirit bear
> The uncreated beam ?
>
> There is a way for man to rise
> To that sublime abode :—
> An offering and a sacrifice,
> A Holy Spirit's energies,
> An Advocate with God—

THE CHRISTIAN APPREHENSION OF GOD

> These, these prepare us for the sight
>   Of Holiness above :
> The sons of ignorance and night
> May dwell in the eternal Light,
>   Through the eternal Love.

CHAPTER VII
THE LOVE OF GOD

When we turn from the study of the Divine holiness or righteousness to the Divine love, most of us, it is probable, are conscious of a certain change of atmosphere. It is not that love runs counter to holiness, or that holiness places impediments in the way of love. But the duality of contrasted aspects is not to be denied. And how often in reflecting upon Christianity we come up against something of the same kind! Thus the revelation of God in Christ is universal in meaning, yet it is also wholly individual in appeal. The Kingdom of God is apprehended as transcendent over the course of history, as a reality to which temporal forms are inadequate, yet it is being actualized through the events of time. Sin is voluntary, but it is constitutional as well, and neither view of it can be resolved transparently, or without remainder, into the other. Christ is human, but it is with a Divine humanity. This is what has been called the " double polarity " of Christian religion ; the fact, in other words, that our thinking about it is obliged ever to swing between two absolute points of view, each of which insists on being recognized as valid, yet both of which we never quite succeed in envisaging as merged in a thorough-going unity. Take any true religious conception and think it out to its logical issue, and you will at last find it confronted by a religious conception not less true because answering just as much to a genuine interest in the believing mind.

That certainly is the case with our Christian apprehension of God. Not merely is there a contrast—and a contrast which is not fatal but vital—between Holy Love on the one hand and on the other Almighty Power, but within the complex notion of Holy Love there is the inescapable contrast between Love and Holiness. That duality is in no sense a weakness for Christian thinking; it is a strength rather, a richness, a fidelity to the living strain and stress of the devout experience. In a recent essay, an English theologian has put in a convincing plea for the retention of this dual manner of interpretation. " The limitations of the human mind and the facts of revelation alike," he writes, " require that the content of the idea of God should be formulated under a variety of aspects. No true simplification is effected by attempts to reduce the diversity of our religious experience, or to submerge under the dominance of any one idea the diversity of Divine attributes which reflect that experience. Moreover, Christian theism, as the trustee of all religious revelation, bears witness to a fundamental duality running through all our experience of God; and the contrasts which this experience implies are ultimately irreducible facts, of which theology is bound to take account. These considerations impress themselves upon the mind

THE LOVE OF GOD

in a great variety of ways. God guides the stars, and He also touches the heart. He embraces all the worlds and He is also the Voice that speaks in Jesus Christ. He is to be known in His cosmic relations through the severe impersonal studies of science and philosophy. Yet He can be vividly known to each one of us in the penetrating way of conscience and in the hidden depths of prayer. None of these can be left out of account."[1]

An approach to the meaning of the Divine love, it has lately been suggested, may be found by considering the Nearness of God. In studying His holiness, we were led to realize how that great idea opened our eyes to the sublime unapproachableness of God, His distance from the creature, His awe-inspiring separateness from the finite in that "otherness" which, when perceived, brings in upon the soul the sheer distinction of the holy from the "profane." No thought of God could be worthy, in a religious sense, which ignored this ineffable majesty. But in the Gospel it is proclaimed that *this* holy God draws near to man. And it is just because holiness and majesty are of His essence that the Gospel, instead of being an obvious platitude, is the wonder of wonders. He whom in one reference we have no choice but to describe as "high and lifted up,"

---

[1] L. S. Thornton in his essay on "The Christian Conception of God" in the collection entitled *Essays Catholic and Critical* (1926), p. 129. The passage has been slightly abbreviated.

THE CHRISTIAN APPREHENSION OF GOD

in another—and for this redeemed men have praised Him most—is seen to be nigh at hand.

In giving prominence to the nearness of God we are stressing something peculiarly Christian in quality, yet something also which links itself on without difficulty to pre-Christian ideas. Wherever the help of Deity has been sought and found, some positive notion of His nearness to those who called upon Him has prevailed. But in the Old Testament a rich vein of witness will be found. Quite apart from the more general idea of God's omnipresence, the inspiring sense of His nearness lies close to the heart of piety. " What great nation is there," asks Deuteronomy, " that hath a god so nigh unto them, as the Lord our God is whensoever we call upon Him ? "[1] That is the voice of the community, of the people bound to God by covenant ; but verses still more tender relate to the individual. Many of these, as might be expected, are from the Psalter. " The Lord is nigh unto them that are of a broken heart, and saveth such as be of a contrite spirit " ;[2] " surely his salvation is nigh unto them that fear him " ;[3] " the Lord is nigh unto all that call upon him, to all that call upon him in truth."[4] So again in the great prophets : " Seek ye the Lord while he may be found, call ye upon him while he is near " ;[5] " my righteousness is near, my salvation is gone forth ; the isles shall wait upon me, and on mine arm shall they trust."[6] A late

[1] Deut. iv. 7 (R.V.).   [2] Ps. xxxiv. 18.   [3] Ps. lxxxv. 9.
[4] Ps. cxlv. 18.   [5] Isa. lv. 6.   [6] Isa. li. 5.

THE LOVE OF GOD

Psalmist puts it all with strong simplicity: "Thou art near, O Lord, and all thy commandments are truth."[1] A similar idea lies in the background of all references to the covenant: God has drawn very near to His people Israel, in all but inexplicable grace. Through such utterances of the devout consciousness there runs the certainty, which makes all things different, that God is *nigh at hand*, and that on this the believer may rest in hours of need.

But light is thrown upon this conception most of all by a study of its opposite. This opposite, with which God's nearness stands in contrast, is not spatial but what we may call spiritual distance. It is the spiritual distance of God that men have in mind when they feel themselves forsaken of Him, or fear lest they may be forsaken, and cry out in agony. In the 22nd Psalm, quoted by our Lord on the Cross, this idea recurs poignantly: "Be not far from me, for trouble is near; for there is none to help";[2] and again: "Be thou not far from me, O Lord; O my strength, haste thee to help me."[3] And once more, in a later Psalm: "Forsake me not, O Lord; O my God, be not far from me."[4] As the religious man awakens to the fact of his apparent desertion by God, or to the even more dreadful possibility that God is not so much leaving him to himself as striking him down in anger, he finds no more piercing expression for the Divine attitude than

[1] Ps. cxix. 151.　　[2] Verse 11.
[3] Verse 19.　　[4] Ps. xxxviii. 21.

to say that God is far from him. Under these conditions, it is noteworthy, no comfort is ever derived from the—at first sight relevant and obvious—reflection that God is omnipresent. The temptation to deny that God is everywhere does not even occur. But to feel that the omnipresent God has none the less removed Himself and withdrawn from the longing heart—there is no pain like this for the Old Testament believer; it is the acme of human forsakenness. And it is the sense of it which imparts a tone of bitterness to the complaints heard so often in the Psalter. The man who grieves over God's remoteness does so because once he enjoyed His nearness, and the lack of it now brings him to the verge of despair.

Moreover, it is observable that Old Testament believers make no effort to mitigate this pain and danger by bringing forward any kind of rational consideration addressed to the intelligence. Such troubles are not to be cured by platitudes. How often they have led men into sombre Deistic thoughts of a God who made the cosmos long ago, but is now far from all He has made! To recapture the certainty of God's nearness—so we must say, if the Old Testament is trustworthy—the saint must afresh *encounter* Him in special and wonderful experiences, which have power to turn the shadow of night into the morning. At times these are of a more public kind, as when Jahveh interposed to deliver His people from Egypt; at times they spring from, or rather perhaps it might be said they consist in, the heard and answered

THE LOVE OF GOD

prayers of faith. The most profound expression of just such an experience as this last is the 73rd Psalm. There the singer rises up to the very summit of Old Testament religion; he grasps the sublime truth that separation from God is the only real evil and fellowship with God the only lasting good. He has carried his heavy heart, perplexed in the extreme, into the sanctuary of God; and there, as he joined in worship, a new impression of what God is came upon him, the light broke through, and peace flowed into his soul. "When I thought to know this, it was too painful for me; until I went into the sanctuary of God, then understood I. . . . So brutish was I and ignorant: I was as a brute beast before thee. Nevertheless thou art continually with thee: thou hast holden my right hand. Thou shalt guide me with thy counsel, and afterward receive me to glory." I need not labour the point that this supreme insight is closely related to the teachings of the 53rd chapter of Isaiah. For there it is made plain once and for ever that suffering, however piercing and outwardly shameful, far from being an evidence of God's remoteness and anger, may rather prove that the sufferer is the chosen medium of God's redeeming grace. Thus the familiar adage, "Prosperity is the blessing of the Old Testament, adversity of the New," does not after all hold good of the loftiest reaches of prophetic faith.

All this earlier insight into what is really signified by the "nearness" of God comes to its climax, and is perfected, in Christianity as the New Testament pictures it. In reading the Epistles, we can perceive that the redeeming vision of Christ conveyed to faith an assurance in equal measure of both things—the sublime holiness of God and His ineffable nearness to aid and bless. In non-Christian worships, these two (as a consequence of the more or less dim light in which they are regarded) tend to fall asunder and become antagonistic to each other; they are not always purely combined even in the Old Testament; and in the ordinary religious life as Christians live it they may easily part company once more. But in the great hour when Christianity took its rise, they fused in perfect oneness. In Jesus, holiness and nearness are indistinguishably united. The very Person, in whom the unapproachable holiness and loftiness of God is once for all made palpable to human feeling, is He in whom God comes closer than breathing, nearer than hands or feet. "Blessed be the Lord God of Israel," cries the heralding voice, "for he hath visited and redeemed his people."[1] All separations have been overcome. It is the same Jesus who humbles us to the dust before Him as we realize the sublimity of the Presence He embodies, who yet by love lifts us up and makes us to sit with Him in heavenly places. The Eternal, seen and apprehended in Christ, does not become one whit less high and towering than before, but now He is our neighbour and kinsman.

[1] Luke i. 68.

THE LOVE OF GOD

He is come so close, that in the last verses of the 8th chapter of Romans the Apostle can declare that nothing which could be named or thought of —not death, the most feared enemy, nor life itself, nor any other imaginable force hostile to the Christian, whether above or under the earth or elsewhere in creation—can interpose between us and Him. And this is an assurance not limited to particular happy moments. It is an abiding element in faith; an element that does not merely remain, half-ignored and half-acknowledged, in the shadowy background, but is perpetually being illustrated and confirmed anew by the deepest experiences of the Christian life.

The nearness of God has come before us as a general religious idea, admitting of various degrees of intensity, which leads onward to, and prepares for, the supreme conception of His love. To this let us now turn.

The love of God, as pictured in the New Testament, is in real measure a distinctively Christian idea. The new faith somehow altered what may be described as the atmosphere of some great human words, for although, as Deissmann has shown, the term *agapē* does occur in profane Greek, yet throughout apostolic usage it is as it were baptized into Christ. Now it puts on wings, and soars up to heights of pure and morally redemptive passion elsewhere unknown and unsuspected. The God of Plato is benevolent, and in His benevolence creates the world in unjealous goodness; but to those who have learned from Christ what love means, benevolence is not quite the same thing. Græco-Roman philosophy, too, spoke much of love as a cosmic force. In those opening lines of his great poem where Lucretius calls on Venus to aid him in his task, he conceives her as a symbol of the all-pervading vital force of Nature. When centuries after, in his work on the consolations of philosophy, Boethius describes love as ruling from heaven, it is no ethical reality he has in mind, but something as physical or cosmological as love had meant for the Stoics. What he is thinking of is the harmony of the cosmos, the immanent law of Nature, the unifying and ordering principle, analogous in the main to our idea of gravitation, by which the strife of the contending elements is allayed. We have only to open the Old Testament to find ourselves in a different world. Classical antiquity will be searched in vain for a parallel to the words of Exodus: " The Lord God, merciful and gracious, long-suffering, and abundant in goodness and truth,"[1] or to those of the Psalmist: " Like as a father pitieth his children, so the Lord pitieth those that fear him." [2] These were heights unscaled before; yet even so, if we consider the national limitations within which Divine love is confined even by great psalmists and prophets, we shall own that the final disclosure, the last and highest definition of what love in God is and means, came only through Jesus Christ.

[1] xxxiv. 6.   [2] Ps. ciii. 13.

THE LOVE OF GOD

The love of God, in its distinctively moral and spiritual import, was at first scarcely discussed by modern writers on theology. Its significance was felt to be too clear for analysis. Schleiermacher made a new beginning with evangelical theology in the first quarter of the nineteenth century, but his treatment of this central idea is meagre, not to say perfunctory; and a powerful thinker like Biedermann rests satisfied with defining it, in barely ontological terms, as an intrinsic or necessary relation of the Infinite to the finite. It is again to Ritschl that we owe a more worthy and thorough treatment of what, once its illimitable meaning has dawned on us, must surely remain an object of ever-renewed and eager study. Ritschl laid down firmly that the love of God must be thought out in ethical terms and must at every point be contemplated in the light of its supreme revelation in Christ. His influence has naturally had much to do with the fuller attention given it in books written since his time.

Not indeed that Ritschl's own handling of the topic is altogether satisfactory. He finds love itself to be strictly a definition of God; for him, that is to say, it ceases to be an attribute and becomes the essence of Deity. " God is love " defines the Most High. Even the concept of personality comes in here by way of what may be called secondary determination; when we inspect the thought of love, asking how much it implies, we instantly discover that it implies personal being, which therefore we predicate of God.

THE CHRISTIAN APPREHENSION OF GOD

But this is to drive in the nail so hard as to split the wood. Ritschl's view has not prevailed, and for that we can see good reason. " God " and " love " cannot be read simply as an equation. Love, it will be granted, is the bestowal of self; but if so, the self that gives must form the *prius* or ultimate fountain of such self-giving. Love, in other words, is conceivable and real only as an expression of personality; and such an expression as does not create, but presupposes, the personality which is expressed. It takes two to make a quarrel, we say colloquially; in the same way it takes two to love. These last words are virtually a quotation from a fine passage in the Gifford Lectures of Professor Pringle-Pattison, in which he is insisting upon the testimony of the religious consciousness to the relative independence and " otherness " of selves. But the passage is implicitly an argument also for the point I am making now, namely, that love in God is the attitude or activity of personal spirit, not an element or atmosphere which has reality on its own account, in such wise that it exists antecedently, and in the relation of logical superiority, to the self that feels it. Professor Pringle-Pattison appeals with confidence, as he says, to the greatest experiences of life " to prove the absolute necessity of what I will call ' otherness,' if they are to exist at all. It takes two not only to make a bargain; it takes two to love and to be loved, two to worship and to be worshipped, and many combined in a common purpose to form a society or a people. Surely, as the poet

THE LOVE OF GOD

says, sweet love were slain, could difference be abolished; the most self-effacing love but ministers to the intensity of a double fruition. As in the love of man and woman, so in a great friendship the completest identification of interests and aims does not merge the friends in one; the most perfect *alter ego* must remain an *alter* if the experience is to exist, if the joy of an intensified life is to be tasted at all."[1]

In the same way, I am contending, we cannot hypostatize love in its own right when predicated of God, as though it could possess an abstract reality and were not of necessity the characteristic of the loving self. Persons do not rise out of love, nor do they finally lose themselves and disappear within it. It takes personality to make love possible. Unless the self is there in order to self-impartation—there as an actual, meaningful, independent Ego—love could only amount to an endless self-creation out of nothing. Self-communication has self-possession as its antecedent. Despite the Ritschlian argument, then, we must persist in holding that in essence God is spirit, with love as its living active quality.

This however does not mean that we are not as free as Ritschl himself to place love at the very foundation of the Christian thought of God. So much we owe to the meaning of the New Testament. From the Synoptic teaching of Jesus to the First Epistle of St John there is a consenting witness to the vast and—if it be

[1] *The Idea of God*, p. 289.

THE CHRISTIAN APPREHENSION OF GOD

seriously believed—the emancipating truth that God is love. Christianity alone among the religions of the world has dared to make this declaration without reserve, and directly in view of uncounted facts that seem to prove it an empty fable.

This revelation, for it is no less, the New Testament plainly traces back to concrete facts of history. The origin of the unqualified faith that God is love is as distinctively Christian as its content. It is no spontaneously generated intuition of the human mind, nor is it the hard-won issue of philosophical deduction or induction; it is a revelation, in which God has been at work in sovereign initiative. This is a point at which, our eye upon what is *peculiar* to the Christian apprehension of Divine love, we must be unabashed realists. We Christians have become so deeply accustomed—at least in theory—to conceive God as boundless love that we too easily forget how in thus conceiving Him we are wholly at variance with the vast majority of mankind. It is not merely that they fail to see what we see; they deny outright that what we think we see is there. And one secret of the vitality of the New Testament resides in the fact that in its pages, or rather in the experiences which its pages record, we behold a new conception of God—*this* conception—breaking into visibility. If we read the apostolic writings on the outlook for relevant indications, we can perceive how the Cross of Christ has educated the thought of what love is. Turn, for example, to St Paul's great passage

THE LOVE OF GOD

which, in Moffatt's rendering, perfectly illustrates the point. "Christ died in due time for the ungodly. For the ungodly! Why, a man will hardly die for the just—though one might bring oneself to die, if need be, for a good man. But God proves His love for us by this, that Christ died for us when we were still sinners."[1] St John strikes the same note: "We know what love is by this, that he laid down his life for us."[2]

Thus it is merely a relic of old-fashioned rationalism, so often naïvely indifferent to history, when men persist in talking as if *this* were part of the normal furniture of the human understanding, instead of being what it obviously is— an insight, a conviction, that rose like a new planet over the world's horizon at a definite point in history. To the writers of the New Testament, love is love when it redeems at inestimable cost to itself; and nowhere else in literature, ancient or modern, have love and redemption become ideas which interpret each other, and which apart from each other have no adequate interpretation. To speak strictly, in apostolic thought the Cross is not just one illustration of love chosen from a number of possibles. It is rather a creative revelation—that is to say, a revelation which entails a revision and transformation of every former thought, and raises the mind that has taken in something of its wonder to an absolute point of view.

This of itself implies that in predicating love

[1] Rom. v. 6-8.   [2] 1 John iii. 16.

of God, we must guard ourselves against deriving the meaning of the love we predicate from normal human experience; for, as we have just seen, the new and unprecedented revelation in Christ was necessary to open men's eyes to what love in God can be. In our common relationships love may be of two kinds. It may be an emotional inclination towards another, implying that out of the sought fellowship and intimacy with that other the person who loves gets a peculiar pleasure; it may also be the profound goodwill, not less suffused with feeling, which seeks above all things to promote the other's true welfare and interest. Now it goes without saying that the first kind of love may be wholly or almost wholly self-regarding; and great literature has much to say of the havoc it may spread through life, if its egoistic fervour be unchecked. But the second kind finds expression in unsleeping care, in gifts that bless, in defence and protection from evil. Doubtless the two species of love may be combined; they are combined, for example, in a true mother's love, or in a deeply happy marriage. But—and this is my present point—they need not be combined; and wherever this quite possible separation occurs, love becomes a self-centred devouring passion, bent only on extracting from its relationship the maximum of personal delight, without care for the needs or wishes of the object beloved. Not that the unselfish lover draws no delight from the enjoyed intimacy; very far otherwise. But his delight is vitally

THE LOVE OF GOD

relative to the other's good, whereas not seldom his evil counterpart would sacrifice the object of passion in body and soul to the gratification of desire. These are familiar things, but they remind us forcibly that in itself "love" no more than "fatherhood" is a luminous or unequivocal description of God as He has appeared in Christ. Revelation alone can tell us what in this supreme case the meaning of love is.

Nothing is easier, or more thankless, than to construe the idea of Divine love with a feeble and shallow sentimentalism. By the reserve of His language on the subject Jesus may be taken as cautioning us against misapprehension so unworthy; and it has been suggestively pointed out that in the Sermon on the Mount He makes the love of God not the reflection of man's love, but its pattern. We are told not, He loves like you, but you must love like Him. "Love your enemies, bless them that curse you . . '. that ye may be the children of your Father which is in heaven, for he maketh his sun to rise on the evil and the good."[1] In His life and death the Preacher exemplified the sort of affection He had in mind. Thus, it has been said, "in comparison with what prevails in antiquity and in human life generally the Christian conception of the love of God represents a reversal: love now moves not from the weak to the strong, from the imperfect to the perfect, in order to find there rest and power. It moves rather from the perfect and the strong

[1] Matt. v. 44-45.

to the imperfect and the weak, in order to help and raise."

There is moreover wisdom in the reflection that for the unconcerned religious temper of to-day we might well add something to the phrase, "God is love," and say rather "God, the Holy One, is love." According to the New Testament, love in God is a paradox as seen through sinful eyes. That the Holy One should love as He does in Christ is what reason could never have discovered; it is something whose marvel, once it is discerned, reason can never comprehend. Only through the experience kindled within us by Christ do we have courage to believe that to the infinite holiness of God there is joined a love not less unfathomable. Apart from Christ, reason as we ordinarily employ the word cannot yield the thought of a holiness so pure as to make love to the guilty and the foul all but unbelievable; apart from Christ, reason could not soar to the thought of a love which through suffering seeks for those who, in their clearest hours, are compelled to despise themselves.

It is then all to the good that writers of different schools are to-day calling attention to this paradoxical and astounding character of the Divine love. We need such a vision of love as will give peace to the deeply-agitated conscience. For the alarmed conscience, which has encountered God and learned how awful goodness is, would be doomed to an incurable despair but for the accompanying simultaneous revelation—for both

THE LOVE OF GOD

holiness and love at their highest become visible for the first time in Jesus—of a love that acknowledges no limit. When we are honest with ourselves, we can place no bounds to the utter condemnation we have merited. This enforced verdict, which we know to be the echo of God's, can be met and answered only by an utter willingness on God's part to receive sinners. That pitying love of God the Bible compares especially to the love of a father. Let us not miss the quality of love involved in the analogy. It is a different thing from the love of a king for his people or an officer for his men. These relationships depend in great degree on the people or the men being obedient; treason or mutiny is apt to dissolve the bond. But as between a father and his children it is otherwise. It hardly depends on obedience or unity of purpose whether a father will love his boy or not; and so far from being destroyed by misconduct, a mother's love will often yearn the more over the prodigal whose folly is killing her. Certainly our Lord never shrinks from the homeliest figure that will bring out the unconditioned character of the Divine love He embodied—its pure grace, its simple relevance to the necessities of its object. "O Jerusalem, Jerusalem, how often would I have gathered thy children together, even as a hen gathereth her chickens under her wings, and ye would not."[1] Such a love flows out upon those who have no claim upon it but their frailty and

[1] Matt. xxiii. 37.

need. And He knew what He did in speaking thus, for nothing else will hold up the man whose conscience has been telling him the truth about himself. Unless we saw a mighty current of unconditioned grace released in Christ, we should be unable to bear up against the piercing sense of unworthiness which Christ evokes.

This subduing love of God, to which every page in the New Testament bears witness, is presented to us not merely as the guarantee of pardon but as the abiding pledge of permanent and unsleeping care. "He that spared not his own Son, but delivered him up for us all, how shall he not with him also freely give us all things?"[1] Just there is the distinction between love and selfishness. "The argument of selfishness," says a commentator, "is that he who has done so much need do no more; that of love, that he who has done so much is certain to do more."[2] How true to life that is! How we constantly set limits in thought to what we shall give to those who need us! We measure our resources, and console ourselves after a burst of generosity by reflecting that there will be no necessity to keep it up much longer. Each new gift is a reason for ceasing to give. But God is love; hence the presumption, rather the certainty, is the other way round. He has given Christ, and all other things go in along with that. Men who had surrendered their boys in the War to the nation's need were glad to supply money

[1] Rom. viii. 32.
[2] Denney, *Expositor's Greek Testament, in loc.*

THE LOVE OF GOD

too, and nights on guard, and service with the ambulances; for after you have done the decisive thing, all else is as the small dust of the balance. The mother who has risked life in bearing the child will not grudge the nursing or the sleepless care. Selfishness says: Past sacrifice is more than enough, and now I must provide for my own comfort. Love says: Where are the new openings for tenderness and succour? for my friend has learnt to trust me, and I must never let him down. But should we have known so clearly that this is love's true way, had it not been for the fact of Jesus?

It is more than doubtful whether love is definable; but at all events the effort to describe it must employ certain distinct ideas. One such idea is that of *persons*. Love of a spiritual kind moves between one personal being and another. So that while we may fitly speak of God's goodness to all living things, love He feels and exhibits solely towards those whom the Bible distinguishes as made "in His image," because they are self-conscious and self-determined spirits. Along with this goes the allied truth that, since love can be perfect and consummate only as it is reciprocated, God, if He is to enjoy from without a true response to His own affection, must call into existence beings possessed of independent personal life—beings distinct from Him, yet in nature so profoundly akin that they can find no lasting satisfaction in themselves, but solely in union and communion with God. And this in its turn implies that in

THE CHRISTIAN APPREHENSION OF GOD

creating a world of persons whose love, to be real, must be spontaneous, He is subjecting Himself to freely chosen conditions. He does what from our human standpoint we have no option but to describe as taking risks, for He ventures the possibility that men may refuse the love He seeks. So vast are the issues with which this life of ours is laden.

Again, it is worth saying that love in God must include that element which in experience we denote as emotion or feeling. As Faber puts it:

> God loves to be longed for, He longs to be sought,
> For He sought us Himself with such longing and love.

There is within Him that which finds us desirable for our own sake, which thirsts to impart itself and receive back the outflow of our love. Because He Himself is love, we are something to Him; His interest in man has roots in His being so deep that for it to miss its aim through persistent human rebellion or distrust, results in His experiencing what we can only call pain and a sense of loss. True, we use such words, as St Augustine says we do the term " Person " in the doctrine of the Trinity, only because we have no better. But they are at least a truer and worthier account of the Divine Reality than the frigid and vacuous language not seldom held upon this subject. The Father has at times been depicted as so inexpressibly superior to all feeling that the destruction of the entire human race would not cause one

THE LOVE OF GOD

faintest ripple on the surface of His transcendent bliss. But an inescapable choice has to be made here, and men will mark which side we take. What has been called the impassibility of God is, in some of its most characteristic forms, nothing better than a vestigial relic of paganism. It stands for the feudal conception of the Prince sublime over his vassals, not for the dear-bought vision of the Father. Its philosophical pedigree no doubt is of an imposing sort, but as Christians we are bound to attach still greater importance to the fact that it runs directly counter to the teaching of Jesus' parables, especially to the implicit argument of the story of the Prodigal Son that God as Father is unimaginably better than the best fatherhood earth has ever seen. If man is made in the Divine image—and apart from this presupposition Bible religion is illusory—we are justified in taking the noblest and tenderest things in human life—those " relations dear and all the charities of father, son, and brother "—as a vantage-ground from which we can peer upward into the depths of the loving nature in the heavens. Once cancel the permission to do this, and our faith falls back to earth, like bird with broken wing. The perils of such daring faith are nothing to those of refusing to think worthily of God. So Blake argued :

> For Mercy, Pity, Peace and Love
> Is God, our Father dear,
> And Mercy, Pity, Peace and Love
> Is Man His child and care.

THE CHRISTIAN APPREHENSION OF GOD

> For Mercy has a human heart,
> Pity, a human face,
> And Love, the human form divine,
> And Peace, the human dress.[1]

Even among men we know a love that suffers when we break faith, and waits with longing for our return. How much more is God sensitive to His children's disloyalty, watching their departure with the pain of wounded tenderness! And if it be said that to root this faithful unwearied love so deep in God is unduly to conceive the Absolute and Eternal One as dependent for blessedness on finite lives, we must surely answer that the love of God is in the last resort self-determined, alike in outflow and in objects, so that nothing essentially implicit in its nature can encroach upon His freedom.

But the more general question may be raised: Do you then propose to make finite spirits necessary to God? To reply, we must first know precisely what is meant by "necessary." It is a thoroughly ambiguous term. There is little to be said for the position, taken by some bold spirits, that we should now give up the notion of man's one-sided dependence upon God, and put the mutual dependence of God and man in its place. This is equivalent to holding that if man needs God for existence, God no less needs man, in a reciprocal interdependence comparable to the relation between the two sides of a woven fabric. But faith must and will persist in holding

[1] *Songs of Innocence.*

THE LOVE OF GOD

that while man is contingent, God is necessary; He is indeed the eternal basis of all truth and all value, whereas we mortals "come forth like a flower, and are cut down." No genuinely religious consciousness could willingly deny the truth of Emily Brontë's "Last Lines":

> Though earth and man were gone,
>   And suns and universes ceased to be,
> And Thou wert left alone—
>   Every existence would exist in Thee.

It is impossible for faith to acquiesce in the view that with the disappearance of man, God also would disappear.

But when we pass from these considerations of pure ontology into the warmer and more concrete sphere of personal relationships, we cannot wind our language so high. Given a world of men, created by a loving God in His own likeness, I cannot doubt that Divine love is, I do not say under a mechanical and external, but yet under a moral and spiritual, necessity—the necessity, in other words, due to the intrinsic character of love itself—of seeking to communicate its own blessedness to the needy finite lives that have thus been endowed with being. The great prophet Hosea did not shrink from interpreting God by the yearnings of his own noble, tortured heart. "How shall I give thee up, Ephraim? how shall I deliver thee, Israel? Mine heart is turned within me, my compassions are kindled together. I will not execute the fierceness of mine anger; I will not return to destroy Ephraim; for I am

God, and not man."[1] There is that in the nature of God which forbids Him—which, if moral character is of His essence, makes it strictly impossible for Him—to turn away from the world's need; there is His tireless and prevenient grace. In like manner, just because His love is of this unconditioned quality, creating the worth of its objects rather than awaiting their worthiness, to lose a created child must be pain such as has not entered into the heart of man to conceive. Hence certain dicta of long-past theology strike upon our ears now with a curious unreality. When for example it is said that God could as easily blot out the world for ever as redeem it, we are bound to ask: Could He, if He is like Jesus Christ, who felt that He *must* give His life a ransom for many? And what would be the meaning, save perhaps for Mohammedanism, of a Divine omnipotence which was wholly out of relation to the character we have caught a glimpse of in Jesus?

The spiritual quality we are led by the Christian revelation to ascribe to Divine love also fixes for us the ways and means by which alone it can attain its glorious purpose. Scripture abounds in persuasive human analogies which set forth the working of that love; its modes of efficacy are those of the love of mother, of father, of friend.[2]

[1] Hos. xi. 8-9.
[2] Study of the question how God effectively commends His love to the mind and heart of man by interior persuasion led the Church to its doctrine of the Holy Spirit—an inevitable step. And since the Giver of this new life of faith must be as Divine as

THE LOVE OF GOD

It travels by the pathway of historical and psychological appeal. Not causation but motivation is its medium. Fellowship is established with the human heart by methods which cannot fitly be illustrated by, or compared with, processes of nature. Not by infusing a quasi-physical grace, as schoolmen have taught; not by uniting man with God in substantial fashion, as pure mysticism often contends; not by the predominance within us of some impersonal principle, as speculative rationalism will argue the matter—not thus can love win its way. The love we encounter in Jesus gains our confidence through historical presentation; its approach and method is that of so revealing itself constrainingly within the fields of concrete human life and personality that our trust, our responsive and grateful love, is addressed and persuaded in ethical modes, which call out the spontaneous consent of the free and conscious spirit. Thus men come most freely, being made willing by the grace that has appeared in Jesus. Love's compulsion is mightier than that of nature. It is more fruitful, more profound, more enduring. The buds in springtime are not driven upward through the soil by violence; it is the warmth from the sky that woos them forth. So the soul and Christ are made for each other, like flowers for the sun; and His influence, charged with the power of His death for men, draws out from

He who revealed it in history, Christian thought rightly proceeded to affirm the oneness of essential being that unites the Spirit to the Father and the Son.

thankful hearts an else undreamt-of richness of self-abnegation.

And to what does this recall us ? Surely to this, that the best name for Divine love—the Bible's own name—is *grace*. That is a word which may at times drop out of the religious vocabulary ; it may be forgotten when the almost incorrigible pride and self-sufficiency of which we all know too much have come uppermost, and even the Christian mind has grown stale and unchildlike, so that we need to regain what Ruskin called " the innocence of the eye," and see things anew as if for the first time. But when the fires of religion begin once more to burn and shine, the great word always has to be brought back. Grace is love in its princely and sovereign form ; it is love to the indifferent and disloyal, whose one claim is their need. " Love," one has said, " may exist between equals, or it may rise to those above us, or flow down to those in any way beneath us. But grace, from its very nature, has only one direction it can take. Grace always flows down."

CHAPTER VIII

THE SOVEREIGN PURPOSE OF GOD

My intention had been to treat in this chapter of
" the Sovereignty of God," but it may be better
on the whole to speak of His sovereign purpose.
I make the change, not from any desire to evade
discussion of the Divine sovereignty, which is
a profound and noble theme on which the last
word has not yet been said, but rather because
I feel that " sovereignty," treated by itself, may
easily leave the impression that God is (so to speak)
sovereign for mere sovereignty's sake, and not in
view of some great end. It is a wise and tried
rule of reflective thought that we best understand
a thing by discovering what it is for, and there
seems to be no adequate reason why we should
not employ this principle in interpreting even
the action of God. Comparatively few, it is
probable, will to-day rest satisfied with the dictum
of an older theology to the effect that the end or
aim of God in all things is simply to promote
His own glory. Not that these words are incapable
of bearing a good meaning. But, as they stand,
they tend to suggest a view of God as not wholly
or purely Christlike. And we cannot forget that
when Jesus spoke of the Father as perfect, He
chose an illustration which had to do not with the
self-enclosed interest of the Divine life, but with

God's kindness to man.[1] Hence there is nothing ethically or spiritually lowering in the conception that God is pursuing in the world a purpose which in a certain sense is outside His own being, and involves the good of other beings than Himself. So long as we remember that His purpose, whatever it be, is and must be His own choice, not something imposed upon Him by conditions beyond and independent of His own nature, we shall not go far astray. That qualification is indeed insisted on even by thinkers who assert that the aim of all God's action *is* His own glory, but at once proceed to explain that His glory is His love.

In this chapter the Divine purpose will be interpreted, not as I hope unnaturally, as meaning the Kingdom of God, which He is realizing in time and will make perfect under eternal conditions. By the word " Kingdom " is signified, after the pattern of Scripture, a phenomenal order which gives full expression or embodiment to God's holy and loving will for all His children. Among points of difference between Biblical and non-Biblical religious thought great importance is rightly attributed to this, that apart from the partial exception of Zoroastrianism, we nowhere outside of Scripture come upon this cardinal idea of the fruitfulness of time. Time, even for the leading minds of classical antiquity, tended to be a mere barren phantasmagoria. It was not conceived as laden somehow with Divine purpose

[1] Matt. v. 43-48.

THE SOVEREIGN PURPOSE OF GOD

working out a mighty consummation, the earlier periods throwing their results forward into coming ages, and the *dénouement* of the End gathering up into itself the abiding issues of the whole process. But in the Bible the purpose of God shows as something to be increasingly, even if never completely, realized within history and charged with incalculable significance for the generations. "Eternity," said Blake, "is in love with the productions of time." In the implicit metaphysic of life held by prophets and apostles there was a place for real events that neither Greek rationalism nor Oriental mysticism had ever given them. Time is necessary for moral experience and must therefore be an element of ultimate reality—so the Biblical writers felt with an indefeasible certainty on which they would have been ready to stake life itself. Hence, in that old world, none but the Jew escaped the taint of pessimism. He had faith in a Power that will not suffer the fruits of past Divine achievement to be swept away by the annihilating forces of decay, but in spite of all human vicissitude, and even by means of it, is bringing in His Kingdom. And one great reason why we call Jesus the Saviour of the world is that He once and for ever established this Kingdom, giving His life as the price of its founding.

When we ask how God must be apprehended, if He is the creative agency behind, beneath and above this Kingdom of all the blessings and all the victories of man, we instantly come upon the idea of His omnipotence. Let us make it our starting-point.

No religion can live in which supreme power is not ascribed to Deity. As Tiele puts it succinctly, "It suffices to note that man's religious consciousness has invariably caused the rejection of every system which limits the Omnipotence of God, with a view to preserving intact His holiness, righteousness, and love."[1] Indeed, if we took a plebiscite of the great worships of the past, this might seem to rank as the Divine attribute *par excellence*. And even if we justifiably take Holy Love as marking the very essence of God as Christians believe in Him, it would none the less be a shallow and deeply hurtful error to suppose that Almightiness can now be reduced to the level of the merely casual or subordinate. Holy Love, divorced from infinite power, is simply not what Christian thought intends by God; such a Being, in point of fact, could not elicit or sustain that fundamental and unqualified sense of dependence apart from which faith would cease to be itself. The obstacles offered by men and Nature to the perfect triumph of the Kingdom are such as to be insuperable save by almighty power.

It is perhaps unnecessary to say that the Divine omnipotence lies at the very basis of Old Testament religion. Every reader of the prophets is aware of this. But what *is* worth pointing to is the fact—often allowed to slip out of sight—

[1] *Elements of the Science of Religion*, Vol. II, p. 93.

THE SOVEREIGN PURPOSE OF GOD

that Jesus Himself speaks of this matter in singularly arresting tones. There is a passage in a book by Titius, one of the most rewarding writers on the New Testament, where things are put in their true perspective. "One cannot make an unprejudiced examination of the Gospels," he writes, "without being astonished to find how enormously important for Jesus' view of God was His impression of God's omnipotence and infinite sublimity. I am very far from failing to recognize that in His apprehension of God Fatherly love constituted the central feature. But the importance of this extraordinary fact can be rightly appreciated only so long as one realizes that His view of God did not emphasize the Divine power, majesty, and sublimity one whit less than did the Jewish view, but took the latter for granted—nay more, deepened it and intensified it to the absolute uttermost."[1] Elsewhere in the same book we are told that omnipotence is in a way a compendium of all the qualities in which the uniqueness of God becomes manifest—which is at all events a suggestive hyperbole.

If we inquire precisely how omnipotence figured in Christ's thought of God, we come first of all upon the statement that it is through His almighty goodness that men are given salvation. When the rich young ruler had gone away sorrowful, and the disciples asked in wonder, "Who then can

[1] *Jesu Lehre vom Reiche Gottes*, p. 104; cf. pp. 48 ff. The passage is quoted by Professor A. G. Hogg in *Christ's Message of the Kingdom*, p. 139.

be saved?" Jesus replies: "With men this is impossible, but not with God; for with God all things are possible."[1] All things are possible with God: that is the strongest affirmation of the Divine omnipotence even in the Bible. It takes the almightiness of God to save a man, now or at the End.

But more. God for Jesus is omnipotent in the physical world as truly as in the spiritual. We gather this most clearly from His unclouded faith in the Father's power to do miraculous things. Notwithstanding His sense of the regularity of Nature, to which He gives expression, He speaks with absolute confidence of God's power to cope with every situation, however in appearance fixed and fated by necessity. Such marvels or wondrous works our Lord conceives as tokens and manifestations of the Divine sublimity, which is so great as far to transcend the normal and familiar course of events. God, to Jesus as to the Old Testament prophets, is a God of miracle, because the world as we ordinarily see it is but a poor and scanty revelation of the Father's glory, and there is a fullness in His mighty being which the life of nature can never exhaust. Indeed, it is because Jesus feels Himself summoned to reveal God in His uniqueness, in His unmeasured majesty and resource, that He cherishes a conviction of His own power to do wondrous works. Perfect faith is free to unseal the springs of responsive omnipotent activity on the part of

[1] Matt. xix. 26.

THE SOVEREIGN PURPOSE OF GOD

God, and in Jesus, for once, such perfect faith became a reality. We may well inquire how far we of to-day have lost Jesus' thought of God, in this respect as in others. The concept of a material cosmos ruled by inflexible laws has caged the modern mind, at times even though that mind is Christian; and we look out to the face of God, often, sadly and half-mistrustfully through the bars of the uniformity of Nature. If we listen to Christ, He can impart to us the certitude of an almighty Father wielding all that is meant by Nature for the accomplishment of unspeakably gracious ends. Faith in Him as Redeemer renders sheerly unthinkable the notion of the world as a closed and calculable system of effects and causes.

Of course we must not talk as if the idea of omnipotence had no difficulties of its own. On the contrary, it is full of pitfalls for the unwary. As a provisional definition this may perhaps serve: God is omnipotent in the sense that He is able to realize perfectly whatever He wills. In the lines of the old hymn:

> What Thine unerring wisdom chose,
> Thy power to being brings.

And let us note carefully what this does not mean: it does not mean limitless or unconditioned power. Very poor stuff has occasionally been written by people who overlooked this fact. Thus in his book, *Some Dogmas of Religion*, Dr J. E. M'Taggart, a philosopher of real distinction, expends a chapter of argument to little or no purpose simply because he insists on taking omnipotence as implying power to make contradictions true. Apparently it does not occur to him that those whom he is assailing have never dreamt of affirming omnipotence in the sense of ability to override intellectual and moral necessities. So far astray does this elementary mistake lead him that he can actually write that " a God who cannot create a universe in which all men have free will and which is at the same time free from all evil is not an omnipotent God, since there is one thing which he cannot do."[1] One thing! it would be easy to make a list of twenty things, all of which have been familiar to theologians for centuries. M'Taggart, plainly, is asking for the existence of a finite moral agent or personality whose being shall not involve even the *risk* of moral failure—which anyone can see to be an ethical impossibility, and therefore no real limitation to the power of Him whom Christians call " God the Father Almighty."

Indeed, certain qualifications of omnipotence are necessitated by religious thought itself. St Augustine, for example, points out that God cannot die, cannot be bereft of His own perfection, cannot make true what is false, cannot act in contradiction of His own nature, or the nature of things He has made. Such propositions may have an unduly metaphysical sound; we may therefore add for ourselves that God cannot make

[1] *Some Dogmas of Religion*, p. 217.

THE SOVEREIGN PURPOSE OF GOD

a selfish man happy as long as he remains selfish, cannot force me to love my neighbour, cannot make vice the one avenue to personal goodness. Yet all these so-called limitations of omnipotence are already provided for in the rough definition of omnipotence from which we started. God, we said, is able to realize perfectly whatever He wills. But obviously it is "unthinkable," in the strict sense of that overworked term, that God should will to die or to sin or any of the other things just enumerated. Such things He cannot will because of His intrinsic character. The possible, in short, is determined by what God is, and only so; hence to represent it as derogatory to God that His action should be restricted by determinate possibilities really amounts, as has been justly observed, "to denying that God is Himself a definite being at all, is either intellectually or morally consistent." Thus an omnipotent being bare of all self-limitation — who in the most literal sense was "capable of anything," no matter how bad or absurd—would not deserve the name of God, but rather be comparable to an infinite mass possessed of velocity without direction.

Popular thinking about omnipotence, it is not too much to say, badly needs to be Christianized. Our usual idea of power begins from physical power—the kind of power we exert, or suffer from, in our natural life. It is from that source we get the framework of our conception, even as used in religion; and any moral qualifications are as it were tacked on externally, by way of afterthought. Omnipotence, when thought out on these lines, means primarily, as it has been put, " omnipotence for happiness—the unlimited power to possess and spread happiness." Scores of the arguments made familiar by popular scepticism have their root, not at all unnaturally, in this misconception. People say : If God is almighty—able, in other words, at any given moment to make the whole world happy if He chooses—why are there earthquakes or tornadoes ? Now what the Bible leaves upon our minds is the ineradicable impression that the only omnipotence for which our faith is asked is that of *holy love*. It is not bare omnipotence that the Christian trusts, but the omnipotence of grace. We are not entitled to construct an idea of almightiness which is quite indifferent to moral considerations, and then correct this so to speak in a footnote. We dare not believe, or invite others to believe, in such a providential ordering of the world as makes for comfort, whether or not it makes for character. And it takes the whole of life and experience to shake us clear, even partially, of the lower interpretation. The only right thing, and the only thing which will bear being applied to the actual course of events, is to take our thought of Divine omnipotence, as we have to take every other religious belief, from what we see of God in Jesus Christ. Forsyth has said firmly, but not too firmly, " In the natural, arbitrary, and unregenerate sense in which we understand the word, God is not omnipotent. . . . He can do

THE SOVEREIGN PURPOSE OF GOD

only the things that are congruous with His moral, His holy nature and purpose." He can do all things, in brief, that He wills; and the quality and direction of that will we learn from Jesus.

There are real difficulties in this region, which it is impossible to solve completely. To the end there is a surd (as mathematicians say)—an irrational element that will not work out. But one thing seems clear : it is useless to try certain short-cuts to the solution. One such short-cut is to say that God is not fully master of His own world, because He is only slowly gaining an all-round control of the universe. Not infrequently in modern literature you encounter—at times in pages animated by a noble spirit—this idea that God is becoming increasingly competent as the ages pass. I will not deny that in a confused and barely intelligible fashion the suggestion does point to a positive truth—to the truth that in this world a real conflict of good and evil is proceeding, a conflict which God permits and does not terminate off-hand. But at bottom it is a view of God that overturns Christian faith and renders wholly confident prayer an utter impossibility. If God is now only partially equal to the task of world-government, why should we believe He will ever be fully equal to it ? for in His case (unlike ourselves) there is no higher source of strength or wisdom from which He might draw reinforcement of His inadequate powers. And if this radical uncertainty about God's future must persist, what really trustworthy ground have we for expecting the final triumph of the Kingdom?

We return then to the point that what Christians trust to is almighty love, not almightiness working at random or without moral purposes. There is a principle here, which may be formulated broadly by saying that the Divine qualities must be viewed as conditioning each other. As the "judicious" Hooker put it, "The being of God is a kind of law to His working." What we think possible for omnipotence is fixed by the fact that it is the omnipotence of perfect goodness, not of devilish caprice. When in unguarded moments older writers threw out the notion that God could just as well annihilate the world as redeem it, we have the right to answer: Could He have done so, if He is like Christ? What is the value, or for that matter the logicality, of an hypothesis regarding God's possible action which is out of all connexion with His known character? It recalls the old medieval suggestion that God might quite as well have become incarnate in an animal as in man. Hypothetical theology of that sort outrages reason no less than it dishonours the spiritual insight we owe to Jesus.

In this region the hardest problem for faith is of course the enigma of evil. Hume has stated the dilemma inimitably (as he does so often), in his *Dialogues concerning Natural Religion*. "Epicurus's questions are yet unanswered. Is He willing to prevent evil, but not able? then is He impotent. Is He able, but not willing? then

THE SOVEREIGN PURPOSE OF GOD

is He malevolent. Is He both able and willing ? whence then is evil ? "

Now, if human action has *anything* to do with the presence of evil in the world—and it takes some hardihood to contend that it has nothing— we have a right to restate the problem. We are entitled to urge that man's will cannot be dealt with as if it were merely a physical kind of force, which without more ado can be overborne by a stronger force acting irresistibly. On the contrary, it is a definite though limited reality towards which God must bear Himself morally, recognizing its moral character. To forget this is to repeat the mistake I have been criticizing, of isolating God's omnipotence " to the detriment, even to the exclusion of His loftier prerogatives." Neither the problem of evil nor that of sin is exhausted by setting it barely and unethically in direct relation to a supposedly sheer crushing exercise of Divine power. But instead of pursuing this line, it is perhaps better to consider the crucial instance where we can see the omnipotence of God being brought to bear on man's evil action and triumphing over it spiritually. Think of the death of Christ. God did not prevent the crucifixion any more than He prevented the War of 1914. Christ's death, in one point of view, was the hour of victory for the powers of darkness, but it was at the same time the hour of their conclusive and irrevocable defeat ; for the crime then perpetrated is made to serve the redemption of the world. They slew Christ in order to bring

His love and power to an end for ever; actually His passion set Him on the throne of Saviourship. Precisely the fact that He was crucified has given Him power over men. Here is found the supreme exhibition of Divine almighty love. If therefore we are searching for the typical and consummate example in which omnipotence becomes evident— not annihilating all resistance but actually bending the resistant action to obey His glorious plan— let us think of the Cross. Neither the sin nor the transcendent purpose is unreal, but the sin is swept up into unconscious subservience to the purpose in whose realization there can be no breakdown.

But at this point it may be some will demur: In thus accentuating the supreme rule of an almighty Father over all things, even sin, and in particular His power to employ each event to work out a loving purpose, are you not preaching Fatalism? To answer quite briefly is perhaps impossible. Let us therefore try—still spelling out the meaning of God for Christian thought— to elucidate the fundamental distinction between belief in Fate and belief in the living God.

It is tolerably clear that the term Fate has often been used loosely and inaccurately to denote what is really imperfectly clarified trust in an overruling Providence. If "fate" be taken strictly, it can hardly mean anything except a blind unconscious Force that by inescapable necessity impels the world and every person

THE SOVEREIGN PURPOSE OF GOD

within it to sheer doom. And *this* is as different from the Christian idea of God our Father as night from day. Three aspects of the difference may be noted.

(1) If Christ be trustworthy, God is in personal control at once of the world and of the individual life. There is an all-embracing plan conceived and in process of accomplishment by loving Wisdom, and faith can discern its essential meaning. Whereas fatalism teaches that no controlling hand guides the course of events; everything just happens, without foresight, without care, without ultimate intention. The world, as it has been put, is a drifting iceberg, not a steered ship. No event in any degree reveals the Unseen or has any significance beyond itself. Chance rules all. The trend of the whole is more than obscure; it is such as to fill those who understand it with despair.

Now it may be said with confidence that among human experiences there are some—and amongst these the best and noblest—which no one of ordinarily wholesome temper would dream of referring to fate or chance. What for example has fate to do with a mother's self-sacrifice? One day we meet a lad just saved from a wreck. He tells us that his mother gave him a life-belt, but kept none for herself, and in consequence was lost. To us, and certainly to him, it seems a moving act of loving heroism. But the scrupulous fatalist taps the boy on the shoulder and explains that, contrary to all appearance, it was an unmeaning outcome of cosmic forces, which happened —well, because it had to happen. That loving deed came out of the world as the rising mist comes out of the sea, and with no more significance; and it casts no more light than mist does upon the ultimate nature of real things. Any such interpretation the good sense of mankind, altogether apart from religious faith, will scout as purely grotesque. In like manner, it is vain to explain a fine poem by fate, which, so far as I can see, could no more write poetry than could a dictionary. Above all, you will never succeed in explaining a great human personality by muttering the word "fate"—St Paul, St Francis, Luther, Lincoln, the Lord Jesus Christ. In presence of such lives the conviction inevitably seizes us that they imply something of infinite importance. They are telling us the very meaning of life. They persuade us, swiftly or slowly and yet in the long run indisputably, that through human existence there runs a plan, a plan that concerns and enfolds *us*.

But if there is a plan, originated and backed by the living God, the plan is bound to go through. To deflect or defeat it is, eventually, impossible. It is a purpose for the world which personally we may decline to serve, indifferent or hostile to its challenge. But it will none the less be fulfilled, if not by us, then by better men. God is working His purpose out, through dark times and through bright.

THE SOVEREIGN PURPOSE OF GOD

(2) Again, fate takes no account of good and evil, but God is the moral law alive. If the innermost reality be an unthinking blind destiny, it follows that right and wrong have no constitutive place in the scheme of things. What is more, truth and falsehood have no place either, since our conclusions regarding this or that are wholly unconnected with the truth of our premises, and follow quite irrationally from their merely physical antecedents—with this awkward result, by the way, that the fatalist's arguments and conclusions lose all significance equally with the rest. Thus the cardinal distinctions on which all worthy life is built turn out to be only casual fancies in our mind. When we speak of that which " ought to be," it is a pleasant-sounding phrase lacking all definite purchase on reality. Moral categories in the final accounting have as little to do with the deepest nature of the Universe as economic laws with the game of chess.

Here too we fall back on life as examined by reflection. Like other people the fatalist unavoidably makes the discovery that, if he departs from righteousness, there will be a price to pay. The world we inhabit is so made that it cannot be otherwise. Reality is built on moral lines. The ethical constitution of things, to which the Old Testament and modern poets like Wordsworth have given magnificent expression, is one of those truths that, once understood, prove themselves by what they mean. Indeed, the laws of the moral universe operate if possible even more inflexibly than physical laws. To get ennobling happiness out of self-indulgence is still more impracticable than to thrive on a diet of prussic acid. Sin gravitates to inward hollowness and misery more surely than earth to sun. Thus the fatalist here is simply wrong on his facts.

Again, no help or guidance is afforded by fatalism in a variety of situations which all sincere minds must encounter. Face to face with a gross injury done to my friend, I derive no light or solace from reflecting that all things go by destiny. If from the other side of the street I see a villain bludgeon a young child, my natural sentiment of indignation is not appeased by recurrence to the thought of fate. If I am tempted to steal or embezzle, and am trying to make up my mind for honesty, no spiritual inspiration reaches me from fatalism; for obviously the fatalistic formula will apply equally whether in the event I become a thief or not. It is no more than saying in advance: whichever I do, will be done.

But if belief in fate leaves a man without moral guidance or inspiration of any kind, and at the worst may ruin him, faith in the living God, who cares infinitely about righteousness and takes sides, infuses into tempted mortals a literally inexhaustible store of vigour. William James proposes the definition: " God is a power, not ourselves, which not only makes for righteousness, but means it." As a definition this from the standpoint of faith has drawbacks, but at least it bids us recollect that tried and struggling men

THE SOVEREIGN PURPOSE OF GOD

can reckon on the interest and succour of the Father, and are never left to fight it out alone. There is moral triumph in the certainty that He is at hand with the reinforcements of faithful love. Who can compute the number of those whom the Divine friendship has redeemed from self-contempt, from despairing acquiescence in moral failure ? Who can tell how many have climbed back to goodness and character because Christ had trusted them, and they must play up to His trust ? Could we put limits to what gratitude may inspire of bravery and loyal service ? Go down to some great dock of our seaport towns, and watch the astounding sight of a man pitting the muscles of his two arms against the whole weight of ocean when he closes the dock gates. How can any one man stand up against the great sea and defy it ? Because at his back is the whole science of engineering, all enlisted on his side. Just so, when the mighty surge of evil is like to sweep us away in degradation, all the power of an almighty loving Father, in His limitless freedom to help us, is there to be claimed by our weakness and used for victory. Temptation does not merely work itself out, in accordance with rigid laws, a cold dumb universe looking on. It is all in the hand of God, the Living and True, who knows how much we can stand.

Temptation, that is to say, altogether changes its aspect according as we do or do not regard it as—not ordained by blind fate but—appointed by the Father for our discipline, that we may learn how to help others. To see it in this light makes all the difference in the world. Leave God out, and then our expectations become grey and dismal, like the landscape on a cloudy day, when the woods stand bleak, and the rivers creep melancholy through colourless fields. Let the sun appear, and the river flashes into a golden mirror, and the woods are alive with twinkling lights and shadows, and all the birds sing. To know for certain that the Father cares and watches is the sun of tempted lives.

(3) Lastly, fate is unconcerned about the individual, but an unchanging God is the Friend of each single life. Men are His children, whom He knows one by one. This is a difference between the two which in all great religious literature comes out with a blinding clearness. Fate brings forth the interminable series of lives only to cast them in turn, like waste iron, upon the cosmic scrap-heap; to it one personality and its neighbour are alike worthless and alike evanescent. It is the equity not of love but apathy. For now the man is only a mind encased in a body—a body for a few years situated on one of the continents forming excrescences on the stellar dot called Earth. Fate has no heart to feel. But God is One who speaks to each child of His great family: " I have loved thee with an everlasting love."

In particular, belief in fate robs us, evidently, of prayer. To pray is meaningless if there be no Divine Mind to appreciate our need and retranslate

THE SOVEREIGN PURPOSE OF GOD

or refashion into wiser forms the too often selfish expressions we have found for it; it is meaningless if, when we pray, we are like a man talking into a telephone of which the wire has been cut. Prayer then becomes unconscious self-hypnotism, the courage it imparts resembles the glow of warmth we gain by running fast. Penitence too must go. Why should I repent if my so-called sin be nothing else than the fated outcome of my circumstances and my health? To be quit of penitence may certainly at first seem a good riddance; but it is only seeming, for to part with penitence is to part likewise with expectancy of that higher aid which alone will enable us to vanquish evil. After all, we may well bear the sting of contrition if along with it we retain the thrill of moral hope. But more: the final glory of love departs. Heaven forbid I should even hint that men and women possessed of no belief in anything loftier than unseeing destiny have not loved each other, often, with brave tender fidelity. In nothing has the intrinsic grandeur of the human spirit been revealed with a more pathetic beauty than in its capability of facing, without surrender, even this final menace of annihilation. Yet to be its deepest and most characteristic self, love must keep faith in its own eternity; it must claim, in Tennyson's phrase, "the wages of going on and not to die." *That* glory fades and perishes, if fate be over all. For love has now become the transient phosphorescence of a certain form of organic life, as unpersisting as the forest leaves. All that is finest in human nature, as it flowers in self-denial, stainless purity and honour, has spread over it the blighting vapour of death and nothingness. Prayer, faith, love—these are robbed of eternal and ultimate significance unless the life we now live lies under the care and sovereign pity of the Father.

The distinction between fate and the living God, then, is not relative but absolute. The whole diameter of being separates them in their bearing on the problem of a supreme direction of the world, of the difference between good and evil, and of the cosmic status of the individual. If God is possessed of moral character, still more if His character resembles exactly that of Jesus, His sovereign purpose is in quality the direct antithesis of fate.

Two aspects of God's sovereign rule as we discern it in the light of Christ have now been studied. In the first place, we saw that sublime omnipotence must be at the disposal of His holy love, if we are justifiably to cherish the assurance that the upshot of the whole universal development will be, not pitiful and unmeaning chaos, but the glorious triumph of good. Secondly, reasons were given for holding convincedly that this omnipotence need not and therefore must not be interpreted fatalistically, but in terms of Divine preferential action. Let us turn in conclusion to an aspect of the Divine sovereignty which in the past has evoked the passionate and

THE SOVEREIGN PURPOSE OF GOD

grateful interest of not a few leading Christian minds, viz., the belief that the overarching purposiveness of God achieves its ends, within this human world, by the method of electing grace.

It is of the first importance, I think, that our ideas about Divine election, *i.e.* the Divine choosing of men,[1] should be kept in the closest connexion with experience, and not suffered to wander off into the regions of abstract and unverifiable logic. It is much more desirable that the thought of election should be envisaged in a Christian light than that it should be, in the less profound sense, rational or rationalistic; for everyday logic seems on the whole a rather poor instrument with which to explore even the deepest things in human relationship, let alone the relationship of God and man. In other words, the true Christian doctrine of election has no bearing on any one but a believer. In the case of a non-Christian, it is an idea we cannot apply; there it is, from the standpoint of faith, irrelevant —as irrelevant, say, as British law to a Frenchman. If you find two people living together in a happy marriage, the presupposition of that is that they have chosen each other. Nothing else will explain the situation. Similarly, if you find a man living in fellowship with God, the presupposition of *that* is that the choosing will of God, with whom the initiative in religion lies, has so operated as to call out in him an answering, choosing faith.

[1] Cf. the words of Jesus to the disciples : " Ye have not chosen me, but I have chosen you " (John xv. 16).

THE CHRISTIAN APPREHENSION OF GOD

Or we may put it another way. Faith cannot look up to God and see Him thankfully as the source and only begetter of personal religion in a human life, without going on to declare that the character of God out of which salvation rises—that is, His redeeming love—is not something that began to be when we began to be conscious of it. That love of His is not of temporal origin at all; it is eternal. It is not accidental or wavering in the execution of its purpose, but rather the innermost reality of all things moving steadily and majestically to its goal. So that from the basis of present experience faith looks back, and sees the ultimate fount of all the Divine influences which make men Christian in the unbeginning love of the Father. Each believer can say : God chose me in a love that is as old as His very being, and that choice He fulfilled in time, in my own personal history, by drawing me to Himself. Thus the doctrine of election is, so to say, an expression of our furthest-reaching retrospect, from our present position, into the eternal duration of the Father's grace. But let us well observe : in all this there is nothing which entitles us to lift the doctrine of election—which is the personal confession of an unbeginning debt to Divine love—away from its proper reference to believing men, who can sincerely make this confession, and to apply it, in the negative sense of eternal and sovereign reprobation, to the non-Christian. From the very nature of things, no one could ever truthfully put forward, in his own name, experiential reasons for holding that *he* had been doomed by God to eternal destruction; and doctrines which have no roots in religious experience ought to be given no place in Christian creeds. Occasionally people tell you that at least the doctrine of Divine reprobation and rejection is a model of logicalness; but there is nothing to do with this except to deny it. It is surely a supreme example of bad logic to deduce a Divine resolve to condemn certain souls to ruin prior even to their existence, from the character of a *Christlike* heavenly Father. My conviction, or yours, that God's eternal love has blessed us can never be made a ground for sinister or despairing inferences about other people.

This placing of the accent solely on the positive meaning of election, this disavowal of dark and (in view of Christ) unworthy ideas of God's eternal reprobation of a certain number of men, has at times been represented as a piece of modern sentimentalism. If only your theological nerves were stronger, it is said, you would do as Calvin did. To the belief that God chose believers in His infinite love you would add the perfectly logical corollary that from the beginning He rejected unbelievers, and appointed them to ruin and misery. Why not be boldly consistent, and either accept the negative belief equally with the positive, or abandon both? The rejoinder simply is that Christ inspires in us the one belief—viz., belief in God's sovereign choice of men to serve Him—but not the other. The same distribution

THE CHRISTIAN APPREHENSION OF GOD

of accent, it is interesting to note, appears in the sixteenth century, when perhaps theological nerves were stronger than ever before or since. In Article XVII of the Church of England, for example, under the heading of election, we are told that " predestination to life is the everlasting purpose of God, whereby He hath constantly decreed to deliver those whom He hath chosen in Christ out of mankind, and to bring them by Christ to everlasting salvation. Wherefore, they which be endued with so excellent a benefit of God, be called according to God's purpose by His Spirit working in due season: they through grace obey the calling: they be justified freely: they be made sons of God by adoption: they be made like the image of His only-begotten Son Jesus Christ: they walk religiously in good works, and at length, by God's mercy, they attain to everlasting felicity."[1] The Article goes on to speak of the unspeakable comfort of this doctrine for believing men, and its power to establish and confirm their faith. I have quoted the Article, some phrases in which may have an antique sound to-day, in order to bring out the true religious instinct with which it fixes upon the certainty of the Christian mind that in personal religion we owe everything to God. No dismal inferences are drawn concerning those who are unconscious of any such debt.

[1] Similarly, in its chapter on election, there is no reference to reprobation in the Scots Confession of 1560.

THE SOVEREIGN PURPOSE OF GOD

Nothing is said which cannot be uttered in the voice of personal adoration.

Election, thus detached from all thoughts of reprobation, is a noble and profoundly religious idea. Every follower of Christ is prepared to say, and like St Paul to say with passionate gratitude, " By the grace of God I am what I am."[1] The immovable base of faith—the bedrock down into which go the pillars of life—is the assurance of God's unbeginning and unending love. " Every Christian," it has been truly said, " knows that it is God who saves, and that when He saves it is not by accident, or to reward human merit, but in virtue of His being what He is—a God who is eternally and unchangeably Redeemer." The goodwill that meets us in Jesus is older than the world, and will never cease to bless us; only so can it be the goodness of God. Whenever religious life has sprung into new and daring vitality, whenever the consciousness of grace has become urgent and imperious, the sense of God's choosing love has leapt up in the believing mind and absorbed every other thought. At such a time men sing doxologies: the soul has eyes only for that which God has done. He is the Doer, we are receivers only. His Kingdom and its members are enfolded in the Father's triumphant purpose, and none, said Jesus, shall pluck them out of the Father's hand.

Read in this light, the doctrine of election is obviously laden with fortifying virtue. Such is

[1] 1 Cor. xv. 10.

the inevitable result of centring everything, past, present and future, in the omnipotent love of God. Hope for the individual, hope for the Kingdom of God as the great order of blessing yet to be—all find their basis here. Think of people who are troubled—not as to whether God is love, for on that point Christ is all the guarantee they could ask—but about themselves. They recall their own frailty, their weakness of purpose, their disloyal folly; and in consequence they lose heart. What is going to help them? What is going to dispel their fears regarding their own prospects as followers of Christ, and their future power to aid others? Nothing will do it, all experience proves, but the realized fact that we have an omnipotent and loving Ally, who will see us through and make us more than conquerors. When we look back, we see everywhere the tokens of His faithfulness; when we look forward, it is with the certainty that nothing yet to confront us can wreck the Father's redeeming plan. Here is the true doctrine of election at its work. So understood, so appropriated, it is no far-fetched metaphysical theorem, devoid of inspiration or value, but the core of an overcoming faith in God. " The perseverance of the saints "—that old, weighty phrase—is in truth the perseverance of Almighty God. It was out of a heart persuaded of these things that long since the great words came: " Thy kingdom is an everlasting kingdom, and thy dominion endureth throughout all generations."[1]

[1] Ps. cxlv. 13.

THE SOVEREIGN PURPOSE OF GOD

Hence the inflexible courage breathed by this faith, in many ages, into saintly minds. Calvinism at its best was a Divinely furnished tonic for an age of persecution. It put iron in men's blood, when dark days were shortly to come upon them. In troubled times, when the hearts of many were to fail, the saints were upheld by the knowledge that for each individual soul, on whom the Divine hand has been laid, there is a vocation as real as if he were alone upon the planet. The conviction that God had chosen them to do and endure His will, and that nothing could separate them from His love, enabled these tried men and women to bear their load. Nothing can go beyond such a faith, and in times of need it is the only ground which we feel does not shake beneath our feet. We think of Knox, Cromwell, Milton and Bunyan ; and we realize how often a living faith in God's sovereign purpose has produced moral heroism of the noblest type. These were men, Froude has said, " able in some way to sound the key-note to which every brave and faithful heart in Europe instinctively vibrated. Their burden grew lighter as they considered that God had so determined that they must bear it. They were crushed down, but they rose again. They abhorred as no body of men ever more abhorred all conscious mendacity, all impurity, all moral wrong of every kind so far as they could recognize it. Whatever," he adds, " exists at this moment in England or Scotland of conscientious fear of doing evil is the remnant of the convictions which were

THE CHRISTIAN APPREHENSION OF GOD

branded by the Calvinists into the people's hearts."[1]

Election, then, is a profound religious idea, from which serenity and courage rise. But one point must not be forgotten; it is cardinal. Election, which is the Divine method of extending the area of good, has a universal trend. It concerns the individual life, but it goes further. It is for the ends of the Kingdom of God, or, if the word be preferred, it is for service.

If this be slurred over, the result of course is to stamp the entire conception as radically and incurably selfish. Belief in election then becomes nothing else than a comfortable sense of personal safety and privilege in which the religious prig will wrap himself round with complacent sloth. One reading of the Old Testament prophets is enough to pierce the delusion. In their view Israel certainly is chosen, elected, set apart, but in no sense for her own sake. When the nation came to believe that God had selected her because of her virtues, and could not dispense with her aid, the Exile promptly broke her to fragments. Yet from the start the prophets had never ceased to proclaim that the Divine choice had great ends in view; and, as the centuries passed, the nature of these ends became clear. If election was a fact, or the special education of one people in faith, this meant that Israel was being trained to be a missionary to the world. We can see

[1] From his address to the students of St Andrews University in 1871 (*Short Studies in Great Subjects*, Vol. I).

THE SOVEREIGN PURPOSE OF GOD

that if true religion was to make its way by the medium of personal influence and testimony, not through magical channels, no other method than this of electing or selecting the few, that they might be taught how to bless many, would have been worthy of God. Our Lord announced the same principle in His training of the Twelve. "Ye did not choose me, but I chose you, that ye should go and bear fruit."[1] In like manner, the words were spoken to St Paul at the crisis of his life: "The God of our fathers hath chosen thee, that thou shouldest know his will; for thou shalt be his witness unto all men."[2]

In this consideration there lies a corrective of much popular misconception. It puts new meaning into a doctrine which has often been represented as empty and outworn. The choice of God, which for faith is ultimate, does not separate men to selfish privilege; it calls them to wide and it may be universal ministry. This larger horizon can never be forgotten.

Even the extremer forms of Calvinism, accordingly, were not at fault in laying emphatic stress on the sovereignty of God. To believe that the world is under no supreme control, that there are events in the future which God does not know and cannot rule and overrule, is to cut faith at the root. The notion of such a God, "of limited liability" if we may put it so, reduces life to anarchy, and when taken seriously cannot

[1] John xv. 16. [2] Acts xxii. 14-15.

but alter gravely the relations of men to the Father. All Christians who realize the vast interests at stake believe in the Divine sovereignty; they can do no other, without ceasing to hold a fundamentally religious view of life. Apart from trust in an overmastering Will of Love, what hope can exist for a world like this, perpetually ravaged as it is by the folly and passion of mankind? No: the fault of hyper-Calvinism lay elsewhere. It lay in its conception of the God who is sovereign. As a product of the age of Absolute Monarchy, it tended to make sheer power the secret and the controlling principle of His being. Might became greater than love. But the true Christian apprehension of God is a pure apprehension of His being as we behold Him in Christ. In Christ we come in contact with the last and highest reality in the universe—our Father, perfect in love, in righteousness, in power. Taught by Him who has made the Father real, near and sure to our faith, we are persuaded that salvation begins with a Love which is eternal, and that in the realization of its designs there can be no breakdown. This is no conviction we should hide. Let it be told out rather with exhilaration, as one vital element in Christian gladness and security. Let it be laid down as the foundation of all our inextinguishable hopes for that Kingdom into which through His Church God is calling men—the Kingdom which is righteousness, and peace, and joy in the Holy Spirit.

INDEX

ART, 22
Atonement, 157, 167

BUDDHISM, 20

CALVINISM, 227 f.
Cross, the, 114

ELECTION, divine, 221 ff.
Evil, 210 ff.

FATALISM, 212 ff.
Fatherhood of God, 104, 110 ff., 152, 189, 193
Fear, 29 f.
Friendship, 52

HOLINESS OF GOD, 144 ff., 188
Holy Spirit, 196

ISLAM, 103

KINGDOM OF GOD, 151, 171, 200
Knowledge, religious, 36 ff

LOVE OF GOD, 171, 179 ff.

Mana, 23, 28, 32

NEARNESS OF GOD, 173 ff.
New Testament, 107 ff.

OLD TESTAMENT, 95 ff.

PERSONALITY OF GOD, 118 ff 182
Power of God, 138, 202
Prophets, 44
Punishment, 161

RELIGION, nature of, 12 ff.
Religions and Christianity, 12 f
Reprobation, 222 ff.
Revelation, 34, 57, 64 ff., 185
Righteousness of God, 160 ff.

SCIENCE, knowledge in, 40 f 54, 58 ff.
Sovereign purpose of God, 199

TIME, 200 f.
Trinity, the, 108, 145

UNFATHOMABLENESS OF GOD, 9

VALUE-JUDGMENTS, 47 ff., 56

ZOROASTRIANISM, 200

www.ingramcontent.com/pod-product-compliance
Lightning Source LLC
Chambersburg PA
CBHW051900160426
43198CB00012B/1683